Hg2|Paris

Plaza Athénée

A Hedonist's guide to…

Paris

Written by
Sophie Dening

A Hedonist's Guide to Paris

Written by
Sophie Dening

First edition by
Nina Vlotides

Photographed by
Linus Sundahl-Djerf and Nina Voltides

Managing director – Tremayne Carew Pole
Marketing director – Sara Townsend
Design – Nick Randall
Maps – Amber Shields
Repro – Advantage Digital Print
Printer – Leo Paper
Publisher – Filmer Ltd

Email – info@hg2.com
Website – www.hg2.com

Published in the United Kingdom in June 2010 by
Filmer Ltd
17 Shawfield Street
London SW3 4BA

ISBN – 978-1-905428-39-7

Park Hyatt Vendôme

Hg2 | Paris

How to…

A Hedonist's guide to Paris is broken down into easy to use sections: Sleep, Eat, Drink, Snack, Party, Culture, Shop, Play and Info. In each section you'll find detailed reviews and photographs. At the front of the book is an introduction to Paris and an overview map, followed by introductions to the main areas and more detailed maps. On each of these maps the places we have featured are laid out by section, highlighted on the map with a symbol and a number. To find out about a particular place simply turn to the relevant section, where all entries are listed alphabetically. Alternatively, browse through a specific section (e.g. Eat) until you find a restaurant you like the look of. Surrounding your choice will be a coloured box – each colour refers to a particular area of the Paris. Simply turn to the relevant map to find the location.

Book your hotel on Hg2.com

We believe that the key to a great Paris break is choosing the right hotel. Our unique site now enables you to browse through our selection of hotels, using the interactive maps to give you a good feel for the area as well as the nearby restaurants, bars, sights, etc., before you book. Hg2 has formed partnerships with the hotels featured in our guide to bring them to readers at the lowest possible price. Our site now incorporates special offers from selected hotels, as well information on new openings.

The concept

A Hedonist's guide to Paris is designed to appeal to quirky, urbane and the incredibly stylish traveller. The kind of person interested in viewing the city from a different angle – someone who feels the need to explore, shop and play away from the crowds of tourists and become part of one of the city's many scenes. We give you an insider's knowledge of Paris; Sophie wants to make you feel like an in-the-know local, and take you to the hottest places in town (both above and under ground) to rub shoulders with the scenesters and glitterati alike.

Work so often rules our life, and weekends away are few and far between; when we do manage to break away we want to have as much fun and to relax as much as possible with the minimum amount of stress. This guide is all about maximizing time. The photographs of every place we feature help you to make a quick choice and fit in with your own style.

Unlike many other nameless guidebooks we pride ourselves on our independence and our integrity. We eat in all the restaurants, drink in all the bars, and go wild in the nightclubs – all totally incognito. We charge no one for the privilege of appearing in the guide, and every place is reviewed and included at our discretion.

Cities are best enjoyed by soaking up the atmosphere: wander the streets, partake in some retail therapy, re-energize yourself with a massage and then get ready to revel in Paris's nightlife until dawn.

Hg2 Paris author

Sophie Dening is a freelance writer and editor specializing in UK and European travel and restaurants. She has written about books for Vogue, restaurants for Harper's Bazaar and electric cars for GQ Style. She also contributes to Country Living, The Telegraph and Square Meal, and has previously written about Paris for Bazaar and High Life. Sophie was born in London and has lived in Hackney for 12 years. Her favorite restaurants in Paris are all the ones she hasn't been to yet.

■ Paris

It's just not fair. Like a friend who's talented and good-looking and charming, Paris has it all: not only heavyweight artistic credentials, world-beating restaurants and luxury brands, and a supreme heritage of beautiful streets, houses, monuments and parks, but also the full whack of contemporary life, from street style (whom else do fashion editors emulate but Paris girls?) to dance music.

Paris' tremendous past lives – glorious, bloody, influential – are written all over its face. Yet day-to-day in the modern city doesn't necessarily correspond to all the old clichés, and you'll have more fun, arguably, if you abandon them. That's not to say you shouldn't read Balzac, Baudelaire, Walter Benjamin and Hemingway on the train, nor that the odd night listening to Edith Piaf isn't good for the soul. Anyway, living-museum status is a no-no, thanks to the city's bold architectural, artistic and gastronomic innovators (and premiers with an eye on immortality).

Is the City of Lights supremely romantic? That depends on who you're with and where you stay. In other words, a capital that's a byword for diminutive hotel bedrooms cannot be the definitive city for lovers. Having said that, hedonism is alive and well and wearing six-inch spike heels – even swingers' clubs are hip here, rather than shamefully hidden in the *banlieue*. If food is your big thing, you're laughing: not only does Paris come top for refined classical cuisine and extravagance on a plate, but there's also a new guard of *bistronomique* chefs, who think smaller, more seasonal and more relaxed, but still provide serious gastronomic bang for your euro. And culturally, the city never disappoints: Chirac and Mitterand's big projects are as impressive as intended; arts funding is healthy; and multicultural creativity bubbles up both where you'd expect it and where you might not.

These densely populated streets are where Charles Baudelaire formulated *flânerie* – the knack of experiencing a city by immersing yourself unrestrainedly. The first-time visitor might have to be patient, though, since you've got to start at the beginning. That means the Louvre, the Rue du Faubourg St Honoré, Hôtel Costes, the Eiffel Tower (perhaps the best of the world's ridiculously obvious tourist attractions), the Pompidou Centre, Brasserie Lipp, even Sacré Coeur and its hordes. Once you've 'done' these, once you've bar-hopped around St Germain, picknicked

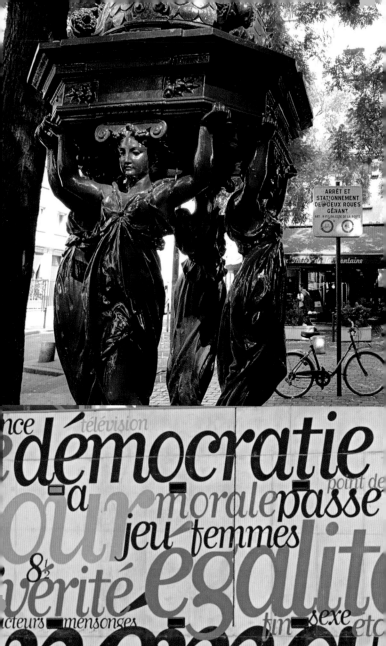

in the Tuileries Gardens and trotted up and down the Champs-Elysées, then you can start to find your own favourite bits. You might start around the Canal St Martin, on Rue Montorgueil with its wonderful food shops, up and down gritty Rue du Faubourg St Denis, the revived Montmartre around Place des Abbesses, and points north and east, such as Châteaurouge and Belleville.

To orient yourself, get a nifty *arrondissement* map, like a London A-Z, only cuter. Paris is divided into 20 administrative zones, from 1 to 20, which spiral out from the 1er (Palais Royal, Louvre, Place Vendôme) to the 20th, out east. They correspond/overlap with the districts known by name as the Marais (3ème, 4ème), Montmartre (9ème, 18ème), St Germain (5ème, 6ème) and so on. Quick history lesson: the Roman settlement on the River Seine was called Lutetia. The Pont Neuf is the oldest bridge in Paris. Molière was the French Shakespeare, and his theatre, the Comédie Française, is still going strong. The French Revolution of 1789 was the biggest and bloodiest and transformed Paris, but there were three more in 1830, 1848 and 1871 (and, just maybe, in 1968). Paris owes its looks to Napoleon III and to Baron Haussman, who designed the broad avenues and the six-storey townhouses. The Belle Epoque was only beautiful for the upper classes. Quick croissant lesson: you can't go wrong with pastries from Au Levain du Marais, Pierre Hermé, Arnaud Delmontel or Stohrer.

As well as immersing yourself unrestrainedly in food and fashion, electro parties and elegant hotels, watch and learn from Parisians, who give the distinct impression that they work to live, that they enjoy eating, drinking and socialising gracefully (just ignore the Rue de Lappe on a Saturday night), and that smoking cigarettes is still cool and sexy. Dear, sexy, glamorous, slightly vain Paris, we know you were the birthplace of the 20th century, and we're so glad you're still incredibly good fun as you charge headlong into the 21st.

Paris Overview

0   2km

CHAMPS ELYSÉES

CHAMPS ELYSÉES

OPERA

OP

TROCADERO
PASSY

ST-GERM

ST-GE
DES

MONTPARNASSE

▞ Sleep

1. Mama Shelter
2. Saint James Paris

🍴 Eat

3. La Fontaine de Mars

■ Drink

4. BarOurcq

● Party

5. La Bellevilloise
6. Chateau des Lys
7. Cris et Chuchautements
8. La Gambetta
9. Glaz'art
10. La Maroquinerie
11. Le Roi René
12. ShowCase

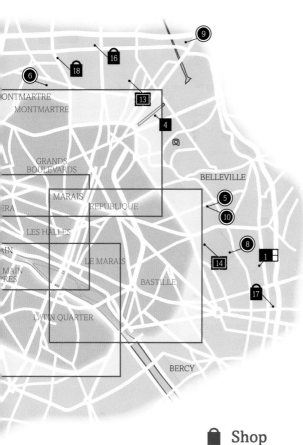

Culture

Shop

■ Louvre, Palais Royal & Montorgueil

The Louvre is mighty. A former royal palace, it opened as a museum in 1793, exhibiting 500 paintings. There are now some 35,000 artworks and antiquities housed in its three wings, Sully, Richelieu and Denon, each with its own entrance beneath IM Pei's great glass pyramid; alternatively, if you buy advance tickets, you can enter via Rue de Rivoli. The entire complex is about a kilometre long, with the Seine flowing past east to west, and the crowds are fearsome, especially around *La Joconde*. For Islamic arts and French sculpture, head to Richelieu, lower ground and ground floors; French painting from the 18th and 19th centuries are displayed on the first floor of Denon and the second floor of Sully.

To the west are the formal Tuileries Gardens, pretty and distracting and full of life, and the Place de la Concorde, impressively panoramic; on the north side, across the Rue de Rivoli are the Comédie Française theatre and the Palais Royal, built for Cardinal Richelieu and serving as a backdrop to Paris power play ever since. This is the historical centre of Paris, the heart of the 1er arrondissement, with smart hotels, offices and elegant shopping on Rue St Honoré and Place Vendôme, plus grubbier retail around Chatelet and Les Halles.

You're most likely to find yourself in the 1er arrondissement by day, in full tourist mode. There's nowhere much to hang out after dark, unless you're doing it in style at Le Meurice or glugging fizz at the VIP Room. It's quite hard to do the *flâneur* thing here; it's more of a mission, whether you're doing the Louvre or looking for an engagement ring on Place Vendôme, where Cartier, Chaumet, Boucheron and so on cluster glitteringly. Stylish boutiques abound, not just on Rue St Honoré and parallel street Rue du Mont-Thabor, but especially around Palais Royal, whose noble arcades have become big fashion-industry news, with Stella McCartney, Marc Jacobs, Acne and Rick Owens opening stores.

Back inside the Louvre complex, the Musée des Arts Décoratifs is one of the most inspiring in the city; and there's a wonderful view from the Arc du Carrousel, along the central axis of the Tuileries, to the Concorde obelisk, the Arc de Triomphe and La Défense. Les Halles lost its character and charm when the great food market moved to the outskirts in 1969, but the area to the north – Rue Montorgueil, Rue Tiquetonne – is mid-gentrification and a favourite quartier for low-key, grownup bars and restaurants, as well as more *flâneur*-friendly streets and shops. The Grands Boulevards, dividing the 2ème from the ninth and tenth arrondissements, are something of a nightlife scene, with clubs and bars like Rex and De La Ville café; half of young Paris seem to arrive by *Vélib* after dark.

Louvre, Palais Royal
& Montorgueil

Sleep

1. Hôtel Costes
2. Le Meurice
3. Park Hyatt Vendôme
4. Thérèse

Eat

5. Drouant
6. Le Fumoir
7. Higuma
8. Le Meurice

Drink

9. Experimental Cocktail Club
10. Dédé la Frite
11. Kong
12. Le Pin Up
13. Au Rocher de Cancale
14. Le Rubis

Snack

15. Angelina's
16. Le Café
17. Cafés et Thés Verlet

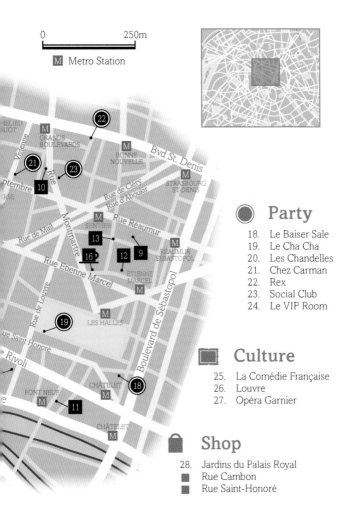

0   250m

M Metro Station

Party

18. Le Baiser Sale
19. Le Cha Cha
20. Les Chandelles
21. Chez Carman
22. Rex
23. Social Club
24. Le VIP Room

Culture

25. La Comédie Française
26. Louvre
27. Opéra Garnier

Shop

28. Jardins du Palais Royal
Rue Cambon
Rue Saint-Honoré

■ Champs-Élysées & Trocadéro

Soaked in money, status and grandeur, the 8ème and western Paris combine smart residential districts with seats of power, major museums and, inescapably, dozens of temples to high capitalism: exclusive hotels, ultra-refined restaurants and luxury-brand boutiques a-go-go. The Champs-Elysées itself isn't the loveliest thoroughfare in Paris, but its wide pavements and chestnut trees sure beat Oxford Street, and recent injections of cash and style mean it definitely has its moments: Sephora, the Guerlain store and salon, Louis Vuitton and late-opening all-rounder Drugstore Publicis are top of our list.

The serious shopping takes place on Avenue Montaigne, also home to Plaza Athenée, that most glamorous of grande dames, on Avenue Georges V, and on Rue du Faubourg Saint-Honoré. Whether you emerge from your spree clad in Lanvin, Chanel or Dior, there's no question of feeling overdressed for a night out. The nightlife scene is hip (Le Baron), fierce (Black Calvados), toney (Le Bar at Plaza Athenée) and trendy (Chez Regine) – anything but casual. The louche clubbing strip of Rue Ponthieu runs parallel with the Champs-Elysées; drinking and partying continues in a glitzier vein to the west, in hotel lobbies (Pershing Hall, Raphael) and fancy dining rooms (Le Cristal Room, Café de l'Homme).

The Eglise de la Madeleine, popular for top-drawer weddings, is a Napoleonic monument with a tremendous classical portico and biblical friezes within. Built 100 years later, a very different piece of quintessential Paris is Opéra Garnier, a riot of crimson velvet, marble statues and gilt, replete with Chagall ceiling and six-ton chandelier. There are several museums around the Parc Monceau area, where the 8ème meets the 17ème, now smart and residential, if not as fashionable as it was 150 years ago; the Musée Jacquemart-André has Rembrandts and a toney tearoom.

In the 16ème, facing the Eiffel Tower across the Seine, is the Place du Trocadéro, where the monumental, winged Palais de Chaillot now houses three museums and a theatre. Come at night to see the Jardins du Trocadéro and Eiffel beautifully lit, or fabulous firework displays when Paris is celebrating. The Palais de Tokyo and the Musée d'Art Moderne are high among the area's cultural must-do's; a walk to the east are the glass-domed Grand Palais and the Petit Palais, built for the Universal Exhibition of 1900 and offering a most splendid eyeful, together with the nymphed and cherubed Pont Alexandre III and Les Invalides, over the Seine.

Champs-Élysées & Trocadéro

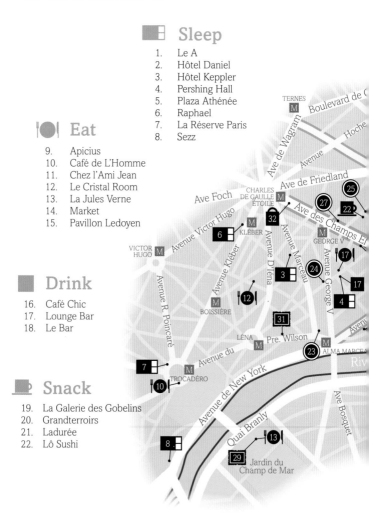

Sleep

Eat

Drink

Snack

Party

23. Le Baron
24. Black Calvados
25. Hustler Club Paris
26. Pink Paradise
27. Queen
28. Le Regine

Culture

29. Eiffel Tower
30. Le Jeu de Paume
31. Palais de Tokyo

Shop

- Avenue des Champs Elysées
- Faubourg-Saint-Honoré
- Avenue Montaigne
32. Drugstore Publicis

Left Bank & Latin Quarter

If you're hooked on Paris-as-movie-set, the Left Bank is your patch. It's bohemian and relaxed, relative to the swanky turf north of the Seine, but really as safe and old-school as an ageing champagne socialist. Its narrow streets and 17th-century *hôtels particuliers* are honey to tourists, especially around St Germain, though plenty of young Parisians flock here to partake of its wine bars, café terraces, 20th-century art galleries and great bookshops. The shopping is fantastic, too, reflecting the taste-maker intelligentsia who own apartments here.

The 6ème and 5ème arrondissements roughly correspond, respectively, to the areas called St Germain des Pres (named after Paris' oldest church) and, to the east, the Latin Quarter, so called owing to the language used historically by the scholars who have congregated here since mediaeval times. The Sorbonne and the Ecole Normale Supérieure are among its academic strongholds; students still swarm to the bookstores and art-house cinemas on Rue Champollion and Rue des Ecoles, even if they can't afford to live nearby. Other places of note in the Latin Quarter are the architecturally amazing Institut du Monde Arabe, the Mosquée de Paris and its hammams and the Panthéon, a domed neoclassical former church that now serves as a crypt and memorial to great men (and Marie Curie), from Voltaire and Victor Hugo to Jean Jaurès and André Malraux.

Chief among the pleasures of St Germain are the bars and cafés on the market street of Rue de Buci, the boutiques on Rue St Sulpice, Rue Bonaparte and Rue de Grenelle, and the Jardins de Luxembourg, for many the quintessential Paris park,

with formal gardens, lawns, sculptures and children's amusements. The worlds of jazz, literature and arts that epitomised the Left Bank between the 1920s and 1960s have passed into legend, though you can still live the existentialist dream if you want (though not necessarily in Sartre and de Beauvoir's favourite cafés – Café Flore hosts philosophical evenings in English now, and its rival Les Deux Magots is very touristy). Excellent brasseries and bistros abound on the Left Bank: old-school Brasserie Lipp (grand) and tiny Au Pied de Fouet (humbler); Allard for trad fare, Chez L'Ami Jean for revved-up Basque food; Le Comptoir du Relais or Le Timbre, both relaxed spots with seriously talented chefs. Clubbing plays second fiddle to bar-hopping, though the Mezzanine de l'Alcazar and the WAGG cover plenty of nightlife territory between them.

The view south from anywhere on the Left Bank is dominated by the 200-metre Tour Montparnasse, built in 1974, long after the area's bohemian heyday during the 1920s and 1930s. Montparnasse is slightly out of favour, and thus ripe for *flâneurs*; the Cimitière de Montparnasse is a particular must for urban ramblers. The 7ème arrondissement is dominated by officialdom: Unesco headquarters, the French Parliament and all sorts of ministries, embassies and places where civil servants lurk. There's also the fabulous prong of the Eiffel Tower, the Musée d'Orsay (Impressionists galore, and a beauteous building, to boot), the truly romantic Musée Rodin, and Les Invalides with its golden dome and worshipful tomb of Napoleon.

Left Bank & Latin Quarter

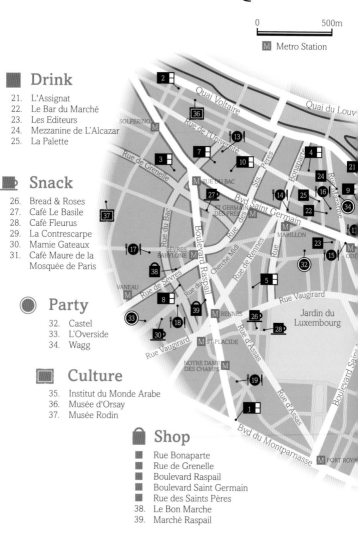

0   500m

Ⓜ Metro Station

▪ Drink

21. L'Assignat
22. Le Bar du Marché
23. Les Editeurs
24. Mezzanine de L'Alcazar
25. La Palette

☕ Snack

26. Bread & Roses
27. Café Le Basile
28. Café Fleurus
29. La Contrescarpe
30. Mamie Gateaux
31. Café Maure de la
    Mosquée de Paris

⬤ Party

32. Castel
33. L'Overside
34. Wagg

▦ Culture

35. Institut du Monde Arabe
36. Musée d'Orsay
37. Musée Rodin

🛍 Shop

- ▪ Rue Bonaparte
- ▪ Rue de Grenelle
- ▪ Boulevard Raspail
- ▪ Boulevard Saint Germain
- ▪ Rue des Saints Pères
38. Le Bon Marche
39. Marché Raspail

▦ Sleep

▮◑▮ Eat

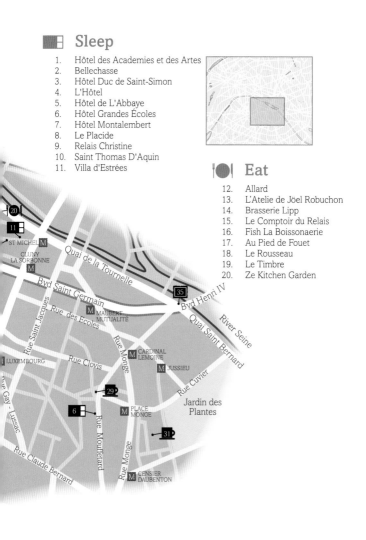

▮ Marais, Bastille & Oberkampf

Whatever else the Marais is and was – Jewish, gay, trendy, squalid (believe it or not) – it was always been traditionally bourgeois and commercial. Its chief attractions today are the pleasure-oriented pace and the intimate scale of those old, pre-Haussman streets; the whole city used to look like this, all crooked alleyways and pretty squares. Grand houses were built here from the 16th century on and, in 1605, Henri IV commissioned the Place des Vosges, whose vaulted arcades remain one of Paris' loveliest sights, pop-art galleries notwithstanding.

Many of the quartier's museums and galleries are housed in the grand old *hôtels particuliers*: within minutes of one another, around the Archives Nationales (itself housed in the Hôtel de Soubise and the Hôtel de Rohan), are the Musée Carnavalet, a fantastic series of 140 rooms full of art and objets telling the history of Paris; the Musée de la Chasse, replete with taxidermy and droppings; the Musée National Picasso; and the Musée d'Art et d'Histoire du Judaïsme, which covers decorative and avant-garde art, the Holocaust, the Dreyfus Case and contemporary portraits with accompanying audio tracks.

Narrow Rue des Rosiers and its tributaries, with their mobbed *falafel* shops, Yiddish bakery and kosher restaurants, is still the hub of the old Jewish quarter, only now it's also studded with fashion and scent boutiques, including a branch of the wonderful L'Eclaireur (see Shop). The best fashion discoveries – independent boutiques, new names, good vintage, Isabel Marant, Christophe Lemaire – are to be had in the Haut-Marais, around Rue de Charlot and Rue du Poitou.

The Marché des Enfants Rouges, one of the oldest food markets in the city, with lots of stalls selling scrumptious prepared food, takes places on Rue de Bretagne, every day except Monday. Most of the Marais is open for shopping on Sundays, unusually, especially the Rue des Francs-Bourgeois, the backbone of the quartier. Gay Marais centres around Rue Ste-Croix de la Bretonnerie and the lower end of Rue des Archives: all life is here, from bear bars to girl-run cafés, low-key to freak drag.

West towards Les Halles is the modern-day monument of the Pompidou Centre, designed by Renzo Piano and Richard Rogers in 1977, with its primary-coloured innards outermost. It houses the Musée National d'Art Moderne (see Culture). Due south, on the Ile de la Cité, one of two natural islands in the Seine, stands the sublime gothic cathedral of Notre Dame, and Louis IX's Saint-Chapelle, with the most incredible stained-glass windows.

Bastille was furniture-making central for centuries, and there are still showrooms up and down Rue du Faubourg-St-Antoine, as well as little cobbled courtyards

and passageways to peek into. There are handfuls of indie-kid boutiques and record shops on Rue Keller and Rue des Taillandiers, but the 11ème's nightlife scene, pretty cool in the 1990s, has become a stew of theme bars, with only a few attractive exceptions (China, Chez Paul). The cooler element has fled north to the pubs and gig venues of Oberkampf, where good, gritty, electro/alternative fun is assured: just head to Rue J-P Timbaud, Rue St-Maur or Rue Oberkampf itself, where Café Charbon kickstarted the scene.

For a whiff of the old 11ème, the Marché d'Aligré is a beloved local market, with a covered food market (Marché Beauveau), and a fleamarket. Nearby Rue de Cotte has some great restaurants, including La Gazzetta (see Eat). If you want to see where the actual Bastille stood – no vestige remains in situ – look out for the special paving stones marking its outline, especially where Rue St-Antoine and Bvd Henri IV meet the Place de la Bastille. These days, Mitterand's great glass Opéra Bastille plays the role of whopping great state edifice.

Marais, Bastille & Oberkampf

▨▤ Sleep

1. Hôtel Bourg Tibourg
2. Hôtel Caron de Beaumarchais
3. Hôtel du Jeu de Paume
4. Hôtel du Petit Moulin
5. Murano Urban Resort
6. Pavillon de la Reine

▮◉▮ Eat

7. 404
8. Benoit
9. Le Chateaubriand
10. Chez Janou
11. Chez Omar
12. Chez Paul
13. Curieux Spaghetti Bar
14. Derrière
15. L' Ecallier du Bistrot
16. La Gazzetta
17. Georges
18. Le Petit Marché
19. Le Réfectoire
20. Le Train Bleu

▮ Drink

21. L'Alimentation Générale
22. Andy Wahloo
23. Le Baron Rouge
24. Café La Fusée
25. Café Cherbon
26. Le China
27. Habibi
28. Le Perle
29. Le Petit Fer à Cheval
30. Au P'tit Garage
31. Zero Zero

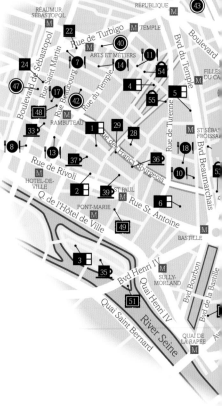

M Metro Station

☕ Snack

32. Le Big Ben
33. Café Beaubourg
34. Café de l'Industrie
35. La Charlotte de l'Isle
36. Le Loir dans la Théière
37. Mariage Frères
38. Place Verte
39. Pozzetto

◉ Party

40. L'Attirail
41. Le Bataclan
42. Le Duplex
43. Favela Chic
44. La Mécanique Ondulatoire
45. Nouveau Casino
46. La Scène Bastille
47. Le Troisième Lieu

▦ Culture

48. Centre Georges Pompidou
49. Maison Européene de la Photographie
50. La Maison Rouge
51. Mémorial des Martyrs de la Déportation
52. Opéra de la Bastille

👜 Shop

▦ Rue Charlot
▦ Rue des Francs Bourgeois
▦ Rue de Saintonge
▦ Rue Vieille du Temple
53. Marché Bastille
54. Marché des Enfants Rouges
55. Rue du Poitou

Montmartre & Canal St Martin

Crowning the 130m hill – the *butte Montmartre* – in the 18th arrondissement, the onion-domed basilica of Sacré Coeur was completed in 1914 and now looms over the touristiest acres in France. Renoir, Van Gogh, Picasso and Matisse lived and worked up here and, alas, you can't move for their commercially minded modern-day brethren offering to paint your portrait. But, even if you'd rather cut off your ear than join the throngs on Place du Tertre, the lanes leading up to the top can be lovely, and the ivy-covered houses, stone steps and general *rus in urbe* vibe (there's even a vineyard on Rue des Saules) are undeniably romantic.

An appealing place to start exploring the 18ème is Place des Abbesses, whose *métro* station is one of very few still to have its original Art Nouveau trappings, designed by Hector Guimard. Follow Rue des Abbesses and winding Rue Lepic up the hill, passing the sort of delis and bakeries that make you wish you had a pied-à-terre, rather than a hotel room. Hang out in a café on Rue des Trois Frères or, by day, check out the fashion and design boutiques and bistros on Rue la Vieuville and Rue des Martyrs, which is brilliant for food shopping. Tree-lined Avenue Trudaine is short but sweet, and quiet for a breather with a copy of *Libération* or an ice-cream. There are two windmills still standing on Rue Lepic; the Moulin Rouge cabaret is on the Bvd de Clichy in Pigalle, which is still sleazy with sex shops and brothels, but also alive with music venues and nightclubs, not all of them grubby.

The Canal St-Martin begins at the Seine, goes underground at Bastille, disappearing beneath Bvd Richard-Lenoir, then reappears in the 10ème arrondissement, at Rue Faubourg du Temple. The streets and squares leading off it are easy to enjoy, especially in summer, when you can socialise waterside, clutching a beer from one of the bars and bistros lining the canal. The area has become fashionable but barely gentrified, and certainly not quite sanitised. Rue de Marseille and Rue Beaurepaire are good for boutiques and galleries; Rue Ste-Marthe retains a hippie vibe; and the footpath is ideal for runners, who can head up to the Parc de la Villette and back, in an act of athletic *flânerie*.

La Villette was given a boost in the late 1980s with the building of a postmodern public complex: La Cité des Sciences et de l'Industrie, a super-advanced science museum; a music museum, auditorium and conservatoire; and a park with themed gardens, pavilions and children's art centre. To the east of the canal lies hip, multicultural, still working-class Belleville, and the beautiful, hilly Parc des Buttes-Chaumont. Away to the west of the canal is the scruffily intriguing Rue du Faubourg St-Denis, with courtyards and passages including Passage Brady, which is full of curry houses, and Art Deco Passage Prado.

Montmartre & Canal St Martin

▦ 🛏 Sleep

1. Hôtel Amour
2. Hôtel Particulier Montmartre
3. Hôtel Kube
4. Villa Royale

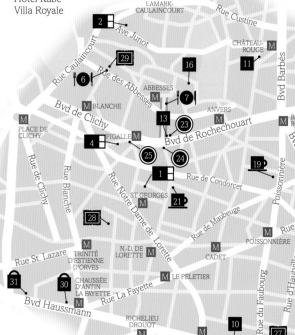

▦ Drink

10. Le Brébant
11. La Chope de Château Rouge
12. De la Ville Café
13. La Fourmi
14. Ice Kube
15. La Patache
16. Le Rendezvous des Amis
17. Le Verre Volé

☕ Snack

18. Chez Jeannette
19. Aux Pipalottes Gourmandes
20. Pink Flamingo
21. Rose Bakery

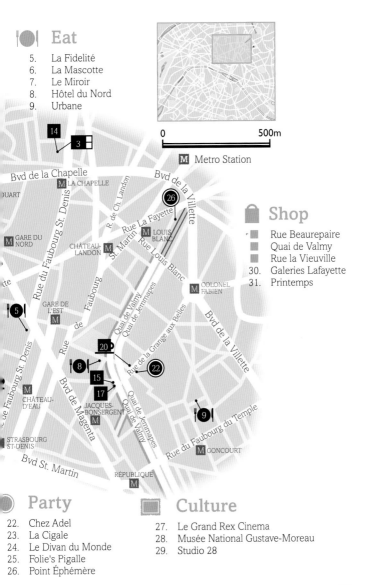

Eat

5. La Fidelité
6. La Mascotte
7. Le Miroir
8. Hôtel du Nord
9. Urbane

0 — **500m**

M Metro Station

Shop

- Rue Beaurepaire
- Quai de Valmy
- Rue la Vieuville
30. Galeries Lafayette
31. Printemps

Party

22. Chez Adel
23. La Cigale
24. Le Divan du Monde
25. Folie's Pigalle
26. Point Éphémère

Culture

27. Le Grand Rex Cinema
28. Musée National Gustave-Moreau
29. Studio 28

33

sleep…

The world's most visited city, Paris is home to some 1,500 hotels, and its association with fashion and luxury is borne out by a real *embarras de choix* at the top end, with desirable addresses ranging from imposing grandes dames and classic ivy-clad boltholes to super-chic boutique hotels and luxury furnished rentals.

Stately and impeccable, the reigning six 'palace hotels' are Le Crillon, Le Georges V, Plaza Athenée, Le Meurice, the Ritz and Le Bristol, all worth penetrating for afternoon tea and an eyeful of gilty pleasure, if not to gambol in an aristocratic suite. Competing at the same level are the historically anglophile Le Raphael, discreetly top-drawer Le Pavillon de la Reine, and cool contemporary scenes such as Hôtel Costes and Pershing Hall.

Many Paris hotels, in particular the antique-filled, characterful gems of the Left Bank, are steeped in history, literary and otherwise. You can live beyond your means, as Oscar Wilde did at L'Hôtel; rest your head in a 13th-century cloister at Relais Christine; or breakfast in a 15th-century tennis court at L'Hôtel du Jeu de Paume.

The boutique-hotel boom that hit Paris ten years ago – giving us arty Le A on the Champs Elysées, Jacques Garcia's opulent, Napoleonic Bourg-Tibourg in the Marais, and Hôtel Costes on top shopping street rue Saint-Honoré – has barely slowed, with newcomers such as arty, irreverent Hôtel Amour in the 9th, Christian Lacroix's pair of fashiony successes, L'Hôtel du Petit Moulin and Le Bellechasse, and smaller deluxe hotels such as Hôtel Daniel and Hôtel Particulier Montmartre filling the 'elegant home from home' niche.

There are bells and whistles if you want them – gastronomic restaurants at L'Hôtel and Le Meurice, great spas at Park Hyatt Vendôme and Pavillon de la Reine, an ice bar at Kube – or pared-down experiences at Le Sezz (no reception desk), Hôtel Particulier Montmartre (no restaurant or bar) and Caron de Beaumarchais (tiny, quirky public spaces).

For the 21st-century traveller who scoffs at hip lobby life and prefers his or her own (ample) space, furnished rentals in central locations are becoming more of

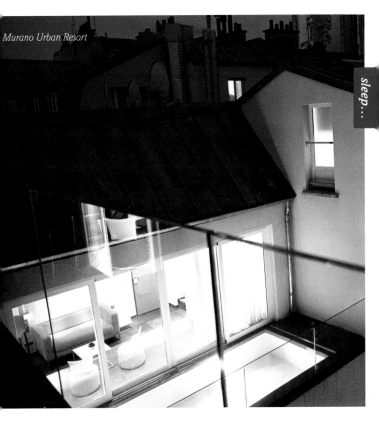

a high-status alternative; La Réserve Paris is at the expensive end, with affordable but nonetheless chic apartments to be found among the edgier arrondissements. These are particularly refreshing if you can't cope with the diminutive proportions of the average luxury hotel room in Paris.

Excellent service is a given among the grandes dames and design hotels; internet access, minibar and room service are standard, with many hotels now offering free WiFi and direct telephone line. Pershing Hall even offers the novelty of a free minibar. Breakfast, however, is barely ever included, and though taking _petit déj_ at the Plaza Athénée may be the ultimate hedonist's start to the day, that hefty price tag is a good incentive to head straight out and get amongst it at an atmospheric café. Be prepared to book well in advance, especially during Fashion Week (first week in October, first week in March).

Rates given are for a double room in low season to a suite in high season.

the best hotels

Top ten:
1. Le Bellechasse
2. Hôtel Amour
3. Le Meurice
4. Pavillon de la Reine
5. Hotel Particulier Montmartre
6. L'Hotel
7. Raphael
8. Hotel Daniel
9. Mama Shelter

Style:
1. Hôtel Particulier Montmartre
2. Le Bellechasse
3. Hôtel Amour
4. Hôtel Daniel
5. Mama Shelter

Atmosphere:
1. L'Hôtel
2. Pershing Hall
3. Raphael
4. Pavillon de la Reine
5. Le Meurice

Location:
1. Pavillon de la Reine
2. Hôtel Montalembert
3. Hôtel Particulier Montmartre
4. Le Placide
5. Park Hyatt Vendôme

Hôtel Le A *(left)*

4 rue d'Artois, 8ème
Tel: 01 42 56 99 99
www.hotel-le-a-paris.com
Rates: €365–660

Boutique hotel Le A is the off-centre, arty result of an inspired collaboration between interior architect Frédéric Méchiche and artist Fabrice Hybert. It's almost completely monochrome inside, with colour provided by Hybert's wall-sized abstract paintings. Dark armchairs and sofas contrast with bright-white cushions; white orchids are reflected in polished black coffee tables and echo the white-painted brickwork framing the modern, angular fireplaces. Tubular lights are suspended at different heights in the lobby, and the calm bar/breakfast area is a celestial South Beach fantasy: white drapes hang over the skylight, and large-scale paintings of trees create an illusion of perspective. The 25 rooms and suites (and one apartment) continue the black and white theme, a ideal backdrop for the artworks and wonderful lighting. Stone bathrooms, pristine white armchairs, fig-scented corridors and a terrific art library attract a fastidiously fashionable clientele; you don't have to wear Jil Sander to stay here, but it helps, as they say.

Style 9, Atmosphere 7, Location 8

Hôtel de l'Abbaye *(right)*

10 rue Cassette, 6ème
Tel: 01 45 44 38 11
www.hotelabbayeparis.com
Rates: €250–520

Located prestigiously in one of the city's covetable courtyards, down a quiet street in the heart of Saint-Germain-des-Prés, the Hôtel de l'Abbaye has been run by the same independent owner since its opening in 1973. Decor is discreetly updated every few years, but remains Paris-trad, with stripes, chintz, toiles, landscapes, busts and well-upholstered armchairs. The 44 rooms are surprisingly spacious, given the densely built location; the courtyard garden makes for idyllic summer drinking, with a firelit bar doing the job cosily in winter. So much love and care has been put into running this hotel, it's hard to believe it carries only three stars.

Style 8, Atmosphere 8, Location 8

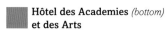

Hôtel des Academies *(bottom)* et des Arts

15 rue de la Grande-Chaumière, 6ème
Tel: 01 43 26 66 44
www.hoteldesacademies.com
Rates: €189–294

Painted white figures, reminiscent of jointed artist's models, accompany guests around this small, stylish, independently owned Left Bank hotel. These and the sculptures dotted throughout play a quirky counterpoint to a sophisticated, warm design scheme employing wood, leather, velvet and satin. The overall effect is contemporary but comfortable, and artistic – the owners' express intention – but not outré. The hotel's Montparnasse location was once the haunt of Picasso and Modigliani, and there's a video-art screening room on the ground floor, as

well as a library and sitting room; visits to artists' studios can be arranged. There's no restaurant, but the salon de thé, Chez Charlotte, competes with the grandes dames by serving Pierre Hermé macaroons and teas from Le Palais de Thés. Downstairs in the wellness room, there's a menu of treatments, including a chocolate massage, on offer to guests till 10pm.

Style 8, Atmosphere 8, Location 7

....

▮ **Hôtel Amour** *(left)*
  8 rue Navarin, 9ème
Tel: 01 48 78 31 80
www.hotelamourparis.fr
Rates: €140–€200

The trendiest duo in Paris (the team behind Le Baron and Chez Regine; see Party) teamed up with one of the Costes family to create this hip young hotel and restaurant just off rue des Martyrs in Montmartre. Everything about it is chic and playful, starting with the pink, adult-rated Mickey Mouse at reception, and continuing

with the 20 rooms, designed by artists and designers such as Sophie Calle and Marc Newson. Each has its own look and feel, so nicely defined you could give them all themes. Playboy Bachelor Pad? All-black walls, carpet and bedlinen, oh, and a million magazines and annuals featuring tanned 1970s model girls. In Teenage Boy's Room, a skateboard casually leans by the bed, and robot toys are scattered everywhere. Some of the rooms have art installations; others are perfect for party people, with bar and private terrace. Bathrooms are replete with Kiehl's products, and Japanese chocolate biscuits wait on the bed. The restaurant is joyously simple, serving burgers and roast chicken, with a gorgeous courtyard for the warmer months.

Style 9, Atmosphere 8, Location 8

....

▮ **Hôtel Bellechasse** *(middle)*
  8 rue de Bellechasse, 7ème
Tel: 01 45 50 22 31
www.lebellechasse.com
Rates: €340–490

Christian Lacroix's second 'couture hotel' (see also Hôtel de Petit Moulin) is a converted *hôtel particulier* with 34 rooms, decorated around seven exuberant graphic themes, from swinging London ('Avengers') to posh Paris ('Tuileries'). The location is definitely posh Paris, moments from the Musée d'Orsay, facing the Louvre, and rooted in the classically artistic Faubourg St Germain. It's intimate rather than sceney: don't expect a restaurant or teeming lobby life; do expect fake fur, alligator, metallic finishes and fanciful wallpaper featuring winged gentlemen and outsized playing cards, sourced by Lacroix from vintage engravings. The rooms are on the small size but beds and textiles are luxuriously comfortable, and some make the most of space by having a bathtub in the bedroom.

Style 9, Atmosphere 8, Location 9

....

Hôtel Bourg Tibourg *(right)*
19 rue du Bourg Tibourg, 4ème
Tel: 01 42 78 47 39

www.hotelbourgtibourg.com
Rates: €230–€260

Jacques Garcia, the legendary designer behind many a Paris boutique hotel (Costes, L'Hôtel and Villa d'Estrées to name but three), has here blended Orientalism with elegant Victoriana and neo-Gothic. Tasselled lampshades, opulent striped drapes, silky fringes and dark-wood furniture decorate all the communal areas and 30 rooms. Narrow passageways and dimly lit stairwells, with their kaleidoscope of colours and textures, conjure up the atmosphere of a Belle Epoque luxury whorehouse. Bourg Tibourg belongs to a tributary of the Costes mafia, so it comes with good-looking, slightly snooty staff, as well as all the necessary mod cons. Its location is a winner, right in the heart of the Marais, and it occupies the same street as the tea merchants Mariage Frères (see Snack). But there is a sacrifice to be made, and that is space: the hotel is tiny, with the smallest bathrooms and lift in Paris.

Style 8, Atmosphere 8, Location 9

41

Hôtel Caron de Beaumarchais *(left)*

12 rue Vieille-du-Temple, 4ème
Tel: 01 42 72 34 12
www.carondebeaumarchais.com
Rates: €150–€170

An antique card table abandoned mid-game, a pianoforte dating from 1792, an ornate wooden harp, an open score on a music stand… Hôtel Caron de Beaumarchais is a unique cross between an 18th-century house, whose owners have only just gone out, and a minutely designed stage set. Lovingly framed collages of old manuscripts and etchings hang on the walls of the rooms, decorated with nothing but the best French wallpapers and fabrics. Owner Alain Bigeard, an antique dealer by trade, takes his inspiration for all this from the quartier's late resident, Pierre-Augustin Caron de Beaumarchais, who was, variously, an aristocrat, watchmaker to Louis XV, spy, revolutionary and, best remembered, writer of *The Marriage of Figaro* – hence the musical/literary theme. The wooden-beamed bedrooms, redecorated in 2008, are small (a Marais symptom) and now incongruously replete with TV sets; Alain tried to resist but decided to accommodate new-fangled habits.

Style 7, Atmosphere 8, Location 9

Hôtel Costes *(right)*

239 rue St-Honoré, 1er
Tel: 01 42 44 50 00
www.hotelcostes.com
Rates: €400–2,900

Fifteen years on from its groundbreaking launch – the mix of sexed-up Napoleonic design and in-house DJs was scorchingly trendy in 1995 – Hôtel Costes is still something of a celebrity, not least in terms of the snooty service, though the clientele is more tourist than A-list these days. Much-copied designer Jacques Garcia created a destination bar and restaurant throbbing with louche, lowlit, boudoir appeal. Reception, guarded by a rather fabulous stuffed swan in a case, is loaded with enough merchandising (candles, the best-selling CDs) to give 'boutique hotel' new meaning. The rooms are brothel-dark and seductive; go for one with a balcony if you can, and don't miss the pool, one of the best in Paris. Incidentally, when you hear something described as a Costes café or a Costes hotel, it is increasingly likely to mean that the fingers in the pie are those of a son or nephew of fiftysomething brothers Jean-Louis and Gilbert Costes – it's not a brand name.

Style 8, Atmosphere 7, Location 9

Hôtel Daniel *(bottom)*

8 rue Frédéric-Bastiat, 8ème
Tel: 01 42 56 17 00
www.hoteldanielparis.com
Rates: €350–€780

Civilised, cultivated and orientally inclined, this four-year-old newcomer to the chichi Champs Elysées is an anthology of orchids, damask, exquisite toiles de Jouy, Kazakh carpets and de Gournay wallpaper in the hotel's signature sea-green. Owing to the exotic antiques and intimate scale, guests feel like VIPs invited to a private home; the lounge and bar are secret, not sceney, and aglow with gilded craftsmanship and coloured glass. In the

26 bedrooms, their walls covered with various toiles de Jouy by designers such as Brunschwig & Fils and Zoffany, bespoke marquetry furniture and Moroccan bathroom tiles continue the well-travelled theme. Slightly unexpectedly, there's a gastronomic restaurant, the chef weaving some appropriately exotic threads through the mainly Mediterrean cuisine. You can also order a steak tartare or omelette in the bar; teatime is a Ladurée/Mariage Frères affair.

Style 9, Atmosphere 7, Location 8

Hôtel Duc de Saint-Simon *(top)*

14 rue de Saint-Simon, 7ème
Tel: 01 44 39 20 20
www.hotelducdesaintsimon.com
Rates: €250–395

There's little to scare the ponies at this charming 19th-century building located down a side street in the boutique stretch of the 7th arrondissement, with its old carriageway door, cobblestone courtyard and antique-filled interior. Taking paying guests since 1904, it's ever popular among old-school romantics (there's a four-poster in the Honeymoon Suite), and the attention to detail is impressive (even the 'No Smoking' sign is hand-painted), though the chintzy, faux-marble decor might not win over avant-gardistes. Traditionalists can bask among austere oil paintings, matchy-matchy textiles, Louis XVI velvet furnishings and flower arrangements; the splendidly clubby public spaces are a real pleasure to idle in. Breakfast takes place in the courtyard in summer, unless you snag a room with a private terrace.

Style 8, Atmosphere 8, Location 8

L'Hôtel *(bottom)*

13 rue des Beaux-Arts, 6ème
Tel: 01 44 41 99 00
www.l-hotel.com
Rates: €255–740

Oscar Wilde uttered his final witticisms at L'Hôtel, and it's fittingly decadent. Given its glittering guestbook (Salvador Dalí, Frank Sinatra, Princess Grace), you might expect a palace preserved in aspic, but a Jacques Garcia revamp put it back in the limelight in 2001. The ambience is discreeter than during its naughty 1970s heyday, but the visuals are wonderfully OTT, with ornate fittings, sumptuous drapes and a lavishly decorated series of intriguing ground-floor spaces, including a major gastronomic restaurant, which holds its own among the top-drawer eating experiences of the city. Each of the 20 bedrooms has its own theme: Marco Polo offers elegance à l'Asiatique, with porcelain lamps and a pagodaesque, wood-panelled bed; Mistinguett is all art deco and mirrors, with a bed and chest of drawers that used to belong to the long-legged queen of the Paris music hall herself. Literary pilgrims can stay in the Oscar Wilde room, though we couldn't enjoy the private terrace and peacock mural without weeping for Wilde's less luxurious last days. The final trump card here is the subterranean, stone-walled plunge pool/hammam, which you can book by the hour for candlelit trysts.

Style 9, Atmosphere 8, Location 8

Hôtel Grandes Écoles *(right)*
75 rue Cardinal Lemoine, 5ème
Tel: 01 43 26 79 23
www.hotel-grandes-ecoles.com
Rates: €115–140

A long-time Latin Quarter favourite, run welcomingly by three generations of family, this tranquil retreat has an almost pastoral quality, as though a modest château has been transplanted into the thrumming metropolis. Three buildings flank a leafy garden where guests delight in peace, quiet, birdsong and breakfast in summer; the impression is of seclusion, even if it takes no more than minutes for *flâneurs* to reach lively Place de la Contrescarpe and ancient rue du Mouffetard. The 51 old-fashioned bedrooms have antique beds and pretty patterned wallpaper, but no televisions – consume some Flaubert in the courtyard, instead.

Style 7, Atmosphere 8, Location 7

Hôtel du Jeu de Paume *(top)*
54 rue Saint-Louis-en-l'Île, 4ème
Tel: 01 43 26 14 18
www.jeudepaumehotel.com
**Rates: €285–560.
Apartments: €620–900**

Distinguished by its location on the island of Saint Louis (cradle of Paris civilisation and, crucially, home to Berthillon ice-cream parlour), this intimate 30-room building is a converted *jeu de paume* hall, ie: a 17th-century tennis court. Apart from the address, its major attractions are the calm atmosphere and a pair of beautiful apartments – highly recommended for living the Parisian dream. Bedrooms are plain and comfortable, rather than sexy enough to be retreated to for the classic dirty weekend, but the historic qualities of the hotel as a whole more than make up for that. The owners have introduced modern features while preserving as much of the original structure as possible, so you get a view of the 17th-century timber roof from the glass lift. There's a music room with a piano (extra kudos if your midnight recital is of Chopin nocturnes, rather than Chopsticks), and a small sauna and spa area, offering seawater treatments.

Style 7, Atmosphere 7, Location 9

Hôtel Keppler *(left)*
10–12 rue Kepler, 16ème
Tel: 01 47 20 65 05 www.keppler.fr
Rates: €300–1,000

Previously a two-starrer, but recently reincarnated as a glamorous sibling to the Duc de St-Simon in the 7th and nearby Hotel François Ier, the Keppler is more or less monochrome but decidedly not minimalist, rocking lots of pattern, stripes, animal prints and dashes of bold colour. It's harmonious, nonetheless and decidedly discreet: there's no restaurant, and the gym and bar are for guests only. The arty/fashiony books in the ground-floor salon make it a lovely place to ensconce yourselves for tea or a sharpener. Alternatively, book a suite with a rooftop terrace and hole up with drinks, room service and an Eiffel Tower view.

Style 9, Atmosphere 7, Location 8

47

Hôtel Montalembert *(left)*
3 rue de Montalembert, 7ème
Tel: 01 45 49 68 68
www.montalembert.com
Rates: €400–1,370

One of Paris' original boutique hotels, a collaboration between hotelier Grace Leo-Andrieu, designer Christian Liaigre and interior architect François Champsaur, the Montalembert remains high on the chic list. It's in pole position in the 7th arrondissement, near the Musée d'Orsay, the boutiques of the rue du Bac and Le Bon Marché department store. The hotel does suffer from Left Bank Syndrome in terms of clunky, contortingly tiny lifts but, luckily, the 56 rooms are more expansive. All are individually decorated, in one of two equally restrained styles: a classical, sandy-beige Empire look, with vintage prints in gilded frames; and grey-toned minimalism, with black-framed photography and modern furniture. Staff wear chic, pared-down uniforms, and there's a restaurant and bar where you can toy with health-conscious tasting plates.

Style 8, Atmosphere 8, Location 8

Hôtel Particulier Montmartre *(right)*
23 avenue Junot, 18ème
Tel: 01 53 41 81 40
Rates: €290–590

This hard-to-find Directoire-style townhouse is beyond cool; it's a work of art, and all the more prestigious an address for having just five suites, each designed by a different contemporary artist. Once you've checked out the conceptual art and interactive installations (less futuristic, more psychological), you can simply luxuriate in the spaciousness, comfort and undeniable charm. It's all enviable: the lobby/bar with its fashion/design library and mid-century modern chairs; the priceless 600sq/m garden, designed by Louis Bénech of Tuileries fame; the century-old *petanque* piste; the toney location. Basically, any hotel that plays Bach cello suites in the bar, and calls its suites things like 'Tree With Ears' and 'Curtain of Hair' is fine by us.

Style, 9, Atmosphere 9, Location 9

Hôtel du Petit Moulin *(bottom)*
29–31 rue de Poitou, 3ème
Tel: 01 42 74 10 10
www.hoteldupetitmoulin.com
Rates: €190–350

Completely adorable, from original gilded ceilings to spiffy polka-dot carpets, the Hôtel du Petit Moulin occupies the façade of two listed buildings in the Marais: an old hotel and an even older *boulangerie*, where Victor Hugo allegedly bought his brioches. Couturier Christian Lacroix has decorated the hotel in a kaleidoscope of genres and eras, creating a chic fairyland of deep shagpile, antique wallpapers, oversized fashion sketches and lots and lots of colour. The rooms provide endless oohs and ahs and the bathrooms are well up to the most refined expectations. Exuberant as it is, it's not for social show-offs; it's a cosy, secret-feeling bolthole, with a guests-only bar, done up wittily with a mixed collection of

designer chairs, bright Formica tables and a petite zinc-topped bar.

Style 9, Atmosphere 8, Location 9

....

Kube Hotel *(left)*
1–5 passage Ruelle, 18ème
Tel: 01 42 05 20 00
www.kubehotel.com
Rates: €210–900

The team behind Murano Urban Resort have created in Hotel Kube another uber-conceptual pad, in a similarly unexplored (by hoteliers) location. Hidden behind gates off a little street near the railway line, it's 100 per cent cool and modern, from the reception desk in a big glass cube in the courtyard, to the bright, white bedrooms off dark, dark corridors, illuminated only by subtle LED lights. Design-conscious and fun (we like the Toblerone and penny sweets), the rooms feature woven nylon flooring, synthetic fur curtains, bedside tables like giant ice-cubes, and photographs of models in bikinis and fur coats. The furry, chilly, trendy-Eskimo theme is carried through in the hotel's brrr-inducing USP, the Ice Kube bar by Grey Goose, where you can sip vodka in sub-zero temperatures, wearing a special anorak. It's all very witty, and as far from the 'toile and afternoon tea' hotels as you can get; this is more like staying in a nightclub or a music video. It's in walking distance from the hip watersides of Bassin de la Villette and Canal Saint-Martin, and not far from Montmartre, but a taxi ride from pretty much anywhere else.

Style 8, Atmosphere 8, Location 6

Mama Shelter *(right)*
109 rue de Bagnolet, 20ème
Tel: 01 43 48 48 48
www.mamashelter.com
Rates €79–249

New Paris hotel in affordable-yet-hip shock! This former multistorey-car-park site (gritty, sustainable, zeitgeisty) opened in September 2008, offering 172 rooms and suites, luxury essentials (great bedlinen, iMacs and microwaves as standard, Kiehl's goodies), and decor by funster Philippe Starck. The rough-edged, jokey design – graffiti and concrete abound – might be chafing for sensitive souls, but if Mama Shelter's mission is to to democratise hip hotellery, it's a great success. The eastside location is a boon if your Paris is more about dirty dive bars than bourgeois bistrots. No room service, but there is a bar with communal table and continuous rolling news, and a restaurant serving trendily unweird food; a rooftop barbecue takes place every single sunny day.

Style 8, Atmosphere 8, Location 8

....

Le Meurice *(top)*
228 rue de Rivoli, 1er
Tel: 01 44 58 10 10
www.lemeurice.com
Rates: €620–14,000

Just over the road from the Louvre, Le Meurice has been supplying sleep to the upper crust since 1835. Though never less than superlatively luxurious and royally expensive, it's no gold-plated time-warp; a 2007 Philippe Starck revamp updated the historic murals and gilded antiques with barbs of Sur-

realist wit (we love the chair with funny little 'high heels' on), and the restaurant, with Yannick Alleno in charge, is among the most adored of the city's dozens of gastronomic dining rooms. The rooms are classical and restrained, all pale greys and lilacs, old-gold damask, marble bathrooms and, in the suites, views of Paris landmarks. The Penhaligon's products are a nod to the hotel's original Anglo-Saxon clientele; the spa treatments are by Swiss skincare scientists Valmont.

Style 9, Atmosphere 9, Location 9

Murano Urban Resort *(left)*
13 boulevard de Temple, 3ème
Tel: 01 42 71 20 00
www.muranoresort.com
Rates: €440–2,500

Keep your shades on, not simply to fit in with the creative-media clientele, but to gaze on the hotel's bright, glass-roofed atrium, its all-white leather sofas and cup chairs and an ingenious fireplace, stretched horizontally along the wall. The 52 rooms are luminous, too, with white walls and carpets and Pop Art prints on the walls, as well as changeable mood lighting. Even the lifts are sparkly. There's an ongoing 'Love&Luxe' package for those who book the honeymoon suite, which has an enviable rooftop terrace with heated pool; you get a privileged 4pm checkout, so you can stay up late on the complimentary champagne and caviar. With DJ sessions and a party atmosphere that's not confined to weekends, this isn't a hotel for early birds, anyway. It's very much a hang-out, with a designer restaurant, two bars, a poker lounge and dozens of varieties of vodka; lots of young Parisians come for weekend brunch.

Style 9, Atmosphere 8, Location 8

Park Hyatt Vendôme *(bottom)*
5 rue de la Paix, 2ème
Tel: 01 58 71 12 34
www.paris.vendome.hyatt.com
Rates: €700–2,500

A cluster of converted Haussman mansions with a creamy-limestone and mahogany interior and masculine-scented corridors (the fragrance was devised exclusively for the hotel by Blaise Mautin), the Park Hyatt Vendôme is something like a luxury cigar box. This is by no means a bad thing: there's a real sense of retreat here, and architect Ed Tuttle's stealth-wealth stylings are spot-on for seen-it-all business travellers and high-status fashion folk. The restaurant/tearoom opens onto an elegant inner terrace; the rooms are impeccably chic cocoons. The slick, round-the-clock room service and serious spa makes the Vendôme the residence *du choix* for demanding A-listers.

Style 8, Atmosphere 7, Location 9

Pavillon de la Reine *(right)*
28 place des Vosges, 3ème
Tel: 01 40 29 19 19
www.pavillon-de-la-reine.com
Rates: €350–800

As if being able to call the Place des Vosges home for a few days weren't enough, the Pavillon de la Reine really does deserve its reputation as one of Paris' most romantic, cosiest hotels. It's set back off the square, from whose loggia drift the sounds of counter-tenor aria or Beethoven piano sonata. A recent revamp has given the communal areas a chicer appeal, with soft-grey carpets, white-gold panels and burnt-orange devoré walls; the 54 bedrooms have been updated, too, and a very tempting Carita spa and hammam installed downstairs. The Victor Hugo suite offers the most space; all 54 rooms have been recently refreshed by Jacques Garcia protégé Didier Benderli. It's the sort of hotel it's all too easy to hang around in, sipping cognac from the honesty bar; when you do make it outside, you're a walk from all the bars and restaurants of both Marais and Bastille.

Style 8, Atmosphere 8, Location 9

....

Pershing Hall *(top)*
49 rue Pierre Charron, 8ème
Tel: 01 58 36 58 00
www.pershinghall.com
Rates: €450–1,070

Thanks to fabulous Andrée Putman design, and a stylish bar and restaurant, faithfully frequented by Paris party people, this small hotel has a big name. Walking in and up to the bar, you get a distinct sense that this is where it's at for cocktails and tunes in the 8th arrondissement; the restaurant gets booked up mercilessly, though guests should usually be able to wangle something (you can eat in the bar, too). The courtyard is a must-see: landscape designer Patrick Blanc has planted an evergreen vertical garden, a wall of 300 different botanical species, lush and thick and strangely contemporary, considering the timelessness of vegetal growth. The 26 rooms, all with Bang & Olufsen kit, free WiFi and a rare complimentary mini-bar, are simple, compared to the glamorous public spaces, with dark floors that bring out bright-white walls and bedlinen. Slate-grey, minimalist bathrooms are replete with Talika products from the hotel's spa downstairs. The American-sounding name is a reminder that you're eating salmon *tataki* with Avruga caviar in General Pershing's World War I headquarters.

Style 9, Atmosphere 8, Location 8

....

Le Placide *(bottom)*
6 rue Saint-Placide, 6ème
Tel: 01 42 84 34 60
www.leplacidehotel.com
Rates: €250–370

The architect/designer behind this excellently located small design hotel is Bruno Borrione, long-time collaborator of Philippe Starck. He has done up the lobby/salon in wood veneer, matching tables and homely but contemporary print cushions; a minimal-modern fireplace provides warmth in winter. Both salon and bedrooms have feature walls in arboreal Cole & Sons wallpaper; refined details include smart white leather headboards, designer bins, deluxe silken coat-hangers and chrome and glass tables. The breakfast pastries are freshly made in one of the best bakeries in Paris, and you are around the corner from Le Bon

Marché, a department store with terrific fashion credentials (see Shop), and a wonderful food hall on the ground floor. In league with Charles de Gaulle airport, Le Placide offers a VIP check-in service, so if you're flying home, you can spend the final minutes of your trip doing some last-minute shopping, instead of queueing at Departures.

Style 9, Atmosphere 8, Location 8

Plaza Athénée *(top)*
25 avenue Montaigne, 8ème
Tel: 01 53 67 66 65
www.plaza-athenee-paris.com
Rates: €595–18,000

The geraniums that festoon the Plaza Athénée's façade are right on-brand, in emblematic lipstick red. It is, perhaps, the most glamorous of all Paris hotels, in a *Sex and the City* sort of way, with the neighbours to prove it: Christian Dior, Chanel and Louis Vuitton all have gleaming outlets on avenue Montaigne. The four-bedroom Royal Suite is the biggest in Paris, with its own steam room and Jacuzzis, a cosmetics minibar, and plasma TVs a-go-go; the view from the bathroom in the new Terrace Eiffel Suite comes and goes at the flick of a switch that turns the window opaque. The furnishings throughout are boudoir-meets-embassy, with velvety swags, fresh flowers and chandeliers; two out of the eight floors are art deco in style, the rest Louis XVI. The cocktail bar is fashionable and fun (See Drink), and the Alain Ducasse fine-dining restaurant truly impressive, especially the signature *baba au rhum*. Seasoned guests and passing

statesmen are more likely to eat in Le Relais Plaza, the hotel's top-end brasserie; Le Galerie des Gobelins (see Snack) is a Claridge's-like experience for tea and cake. Finally, there's the new Institut Dior downstairs, allowing high capitalism's winners to live the dream even more profoundly.

Style 9, Atmosphere 8, Location 8

Raphael *(bottom)*
17 avenue Kléber, 16ème
Tel: 01 53 64 32 00
www.raphael-hotel.com
Rates: €505–6,180

Still owned by the Bavarez family, who built it in 1925 in response to demand for a more intimate sort of hotel, the Raphael is something like an English stately home as imagined during Hollywood's golden age, with walnut-panelled gallery lobby, stained-glass windows and antique tapestries. There's lots of room in the sumptuously decorated rooms, whose high, wooden-arched ceilings, opulent Louis XVI furnishings and whopping built-in wardrobes have been kept spruce with successive restorations. Even if you don't check in, do check out the Bar Anglais for a well-heeled cocktail, and/or panoramic lunch at Les Jardins Plein Ciel, the hotel's swish top-floor terrace. Service is particularly excellent; the concierge is primed with local recommendations for eating and drinking that you might not otherwise come across.

Style 8, Atmosphere 9, Location 8

Relais Christine *(left)*
3 rue Christine, 6ème
Tel: 01 40 51 60 80
www.relais-christine.com
Rates: €380–850

All is calm at the Relais Christine, a charming establishment on the Left Bank that makes the ideal classic-contempary base for an unreconstructed, traditional Paris trip. It's handy for the Louvre, the Musée d'Orsay and the river and, though it's a peaceful choice in itself, it's surrounded by buzzing restaurants and bars – those on rue Saint-André-des-Arts, for a start. You can still discern the building's former incarnation as a 16th-century mansion (built on the ruins of a 13th-century Augustinian cloister), as you approach the entrance through the old courtyard; the resident coat of armour has been here for centuries, too. Try to get a beamed room for extra historic atmosphere, or one with a terrace for summer chilling. There's no restaurant or bar as such, but the plushly inviting sitting room has an honesty bar; and a super spa awaits in the converted basement vaults.

Style 8, Atmosphere 8, Location 8

La Réserve Paris *(top)*
10 place du Trocadéro, 16ème
Tel: 01 53 70 53 70
www.lareserve-paris.com
**Rates: €5,000–€10,000
per three-day stay**

Deluxe furnished rentals are the way to go for publicity-shy A-listers, security-conscious royals and business travellers with children in tow. The ultimate in serviced apartments in Paris, La Réserve has a trump card of particular value in Paris and that is space. Take a two-bedroom duplex with Eiffel Tower view and you'd have to shout to be heard from bedroom to kitchen. The frills are few (own-brand bathroom products, Mariage Frères teabags) but the home office is tip-top, and you can order in *anything*; the concierge service competes with the best in the world. You can invite friends for dinner, watch a Chabrol film in the home-cinema area, and definitely have a bath in one of the best tubs in town. Swanking in and out of your own apartment on the place du Trocadéro is a pleasure in itself.

Style 8, Atmosphere 6, Location 9

Saint James Paris *(right)*
43 avenue Bugeaud, 16ème
Tel: 01 44 05 81 81
www.saint-james-paris.com
Rates: €510–860

A Parisian family bought this 100-year-old château and converted it into a luxury hotel in 1990; it used to belong to an Englishman who ran it a a gentleman's club. It still is technically a member's club, as well as a smart hotel, with a grand staircase and wood-panelled library bar (there's a red pillar box and good old telephone box in the grounds, too). The Parisian elite hold business lunches here, making the most of a restaurant that's open only to members and hotel guests. Many who stay are regulars, booking into the same room every time; the sense of exclusivity is compounded by high walls and the park-style gardens. The

rooms more like huge apartments, befitting the hotel's status as the only château-hotel in Paris.

Style 7, Atmosphere 8, Location 7

Saint Thomas d'Aquin *(left)*
3 rue du Pré-aux-Clercs, 7ème
Tel: 01 42 61 01 22
www.hotel-st-thomas-daquin.com
Rates: €140

This greenery-swathed mansion is a real find, not only owing to its St Germain location but also because it's both stylish and incredibly good value for money. The lobby and sitting room are simply decorated, with light-grey walls, boxy armchairs and dark-wood tables strewn with newspapers and magazines. The rooms all come with chic checked or striped curtains and headboards, French windows with wooden shutters and free WiFi. Aperitifs can be taken in the salon, where breakfast takes place. Leafy, pretty and prized for its peacefulness, the rue du Pré aux Clercs is also home to a new sibling establishment, the three-star, smarter and more costly Hôtel Saint-Vincent.

Style 8, Atmosphere 8, Location 8

Sezz *(top)*
6 avenue Frémiet, 16ème
Tel: 01 56 75 26 26
www.hotelsezz.com
Rates: €330–670

Groovily, at the Sezz they've done away with the whole reception-desk concept; instead, assistants are on call via walkie-talkies, and check-in takes place at the Grande Dame Bar (Veuve Clicquot's house fizz) and involves cocktails or coffee. There are 27 rooms, each unique, but all featuring low beds swathed in charcoal cashmere, rough-hewn grey slate walls (look out for the occasional fossil), and indulgent bathrooms partitioned off by sheet glass. Diverting details include a superior selection of coffee-table books, double bathtubs, pivoting flatscreen TVs, and a hammam and Jacuzzi in the basement. The residential location is somewhat incongruous, considering the fashion-conscious clientele, but the designer cosiness is great to 'come home' to, plus the Eiffel Tower's just a short walk away.

Style 9, Atmosphere 8, Location 7

Hôtel Thérèse *(right)*
5–7 rue Thérèse, 1er
Tel: 01 42 96 10 01
www.hoteltherese.com
Rates: €155–320

Excellently priced, considering its super-central location, this is an unflashy, understated hotel, done up in can't-go-wrong, classic-contemporary style. The communal areas are inviting and warm: the lounge has an elegant, comfortable sofa and armchairs, a cluster of 20th-century paintings, refined dark-walnut furniture and parquet floors. The 40 rooms and three suites are more restrained, colourwise, and dominated by beds with tall brown headboards. There's nothing radical or envelope-pushing within these historic walls; rather, Thérèse's strength is in its address, right in the heart of

the Right Bank, an easy walk from Place Vendôme, the Louvre and rue St-Honoré. In spite of this, it also feels removed, far from the maddening crowds, hidden in a narrow side street down which traffic rarely flows.

Style 7, Atmosphere 7, Location 9

Villa d'Estrées *(top)*
17 rue Gît-le-Coeur, 6ème
Tel: 01 55 42 71 11
www.villadestrees.com
Rates: €195–355

Jacques Garcia designed this tiny, sexy-looking hotel, a bolthole *sans* restaurant on a picturesque cobblestoned street in between animated rue Saint André des Arts, Boulevard Saint-Michel and the Seine. The rooms are opulently masculine, done out in a modern Empire style with silk curtains, striped upholstery and carpets, and bold patterned or striped wallpaper. White bedlinen, and orchids in the bathroom provide brushes with minimalist calm. Breakfast is served in the entrance lobby, an exotic 19th-century cocktail of black and gold paint, straight-backed armchairs and long red-velvet drapes. Directly opposite, also broodingly painted black, the Résidence des Arts offers another 11 rooms along the same plush, good-value lines.

Style 9, Atmosphere 8, Location 8

Villa Royale *(bottom)*
2 rue Duperré, 18ème
Tel: 01 55 31 78 78
www.leshotelsdeparis.com
Rates: €250–660

The Pigalle district isn't all sex, sex, sex – it does sleaze, sauce and showgirls, too. A rock-star pad with wittily whorish, neo-baroque rooms, Villa Royale pays tribute to all of the above, but it's at a sufficient distance from the neon lights, for you to keep things vicariously decadent. The hotel's tongue-in-cheek shtick involves pink silk padded doors, pink drapes, swags and walls, gilt-framed LCD screens and fireplaces, Jacuzzis for two… Each room is named after a glamorous celeb: Naomi Campbell, Catherine Deneuve, Serge Gainsbourg, all of whom conjure up a bit of kinky imagery in one way or another. The perfect place for a frolicsome weekend in Paris and, equally, a good choice if you're bent on exploring the youthful bars and boutiques of Montmartre.

Style 8, Atmosphere 8, Location 8

Allard

eat...

First, there *is* a difference between a brasserie and a bistro – it's to do with Alsace and seafood and professional waiting staff. However, though we've cleared that up, in 21st-century Paris 'bistro' can mean just about anything its owners want it to, so you'd be forgiven for experiencing confusion. The restaurants we've chosen to flag up are largely French, and represent all the current incarnations of the bistro: the old-school classic with brass rails and snails, such as Allard; the poshed-up version, often with a celebrity chef's name on the menu (Benoît, Drouant); and the small, exciting, inexpensive neo-bistro, such as Châteaubriand, Urbane and Le Timbre, where the food's the thing, and humble ingredients are key.

The move away from foie gras and lobster, classical sauces and ponderous service isn't a new thing; big-name chefs began to launch diffusion-line type ventures back in the early 1990s, and Le Fooding – a movement, not just a website – has been bringing fresh thinking to the Paris food scene for 10 years. The current crop of hot young chefs are influenced by neo-bistro pioneers like Yves Camdeborde, whose Comptoir du Relais in St-Germain has, at the time of going to press, the hottest tables in town.

That is not to say that you should come to Paris without getting some haute cuisine action. The most admired are Yannick Alléno at Le Meurice, Eric Fréchon at Le Bristol, Alain Ducasse at Plaza Athenée, Les Ambassadeurs at Hôtel de Crillon, Le Restaurant at L'Hôtel – and those are just the hotel dining rooms. Needless to say, these are eating experiences that don't come cheap. Just a little further down the food chain, but still ultra-glamorous, are stylish, upscale haunts such as L'Atelier de Jöel Robuchon, Market and Georges, where you can nibble, rather than going all-in; tapas and sushi have definitely made their mark on Paris.

Lower-key favourites abound, from the café-brasserie (Le Fumoir) to the good-value local, which might be trendy and youthful (Le Réfectoire, Hôtel du Nord) or honest and old-fashioned (Chez Paul, Chez Janou). Cheap eats are more likely among the non-French quarters: Chinese in the 20th and 13th arrondissement, Japanese around the Rue Ste-Anne in the 2ème, and Middle Eastern and North African all over the city. Modern bistros tend not to be cheap, though the quality of the ingredients and cooking mean you get a top deal for your money. The buzz around smaller 'chef's bistros' guarantees a fun atmosphere and a cool crowd, too.

There's a funny side to all the innovation going on around the Paris food scene. Shifting habits are seeing Parisians abandoning the daily three-course lunch and seeking snackier options; an English influence is clearly at work, going by the success of Rose Bakery and Bread & Roses (see Snack). Increased respect for suppliers and seasonality, so key to the British food renaissance of recent years, is taking hold in France, too. Fancy that.

Some things, though, will never change. For the most part, eating takes place strictly between noon and 2.30pm, and 8pm and 10.30pm. Booking is always advised.

Prices given are for two courses and half a bottle of wine for one.

Le Comptoir du Relais

the best restaurants

Top ten:
1. Le Comptoir du Relais
2. Le Timbre
3. Le Café de l'Homme
4. Le Meurice
5. Ze Kitchen Galerie
6. Le Jules Verne
7. Le Châteaubriand
8. L'Atelier de Joël Robuchon
9. Derrière
10. Chez Janou

Food:
1. Le Meurice
2. Le Timbre
3. Le Pavillon Ledoyen
4. Le Châteaubriand
5. Ze Kitchen Galerie

Service:
1. Drouant
2. Le Réfectoire
3. Allard
4. Apicius
5. Le Meurice

Atmosphere:
1. Derrière
2. Chez Janou
3. L'Ecailler du Bistrot
4. Le Comptoir du Relais
5. Le Café de l'Homme

404 *(bottom)*

69 rue des Gravilliers, 3ème
Tel: 01 42 74 57 81
Open: daily, noon–2.30pm (4pm Sat–Sun), 8pm–midnight
North African €50

404, named nomadically after the antique Peugeot 404 (a legend in Morocco), is full of the off-kilter charm that's virtually a trademark of its owner, Mourad Mazouz. Like his Momo in London, it's an uncomplicated but celebtastic North African eatery with something of a party atmosphere by night, and a fun next-door neighbour in cocktail bar Andy Wahloo, where you can continue on the mojitos, post-tagine. 404 is small, dark and cosy, a Berber cave with bare stone walls, imported carvings and lanterns, and waiters who give it lots of cheerful energy. Everything on the traditional menu is terrific, with the fish *tagine* and the *couscous méchoui*, aka Maghrebi-style roast lamb, our most-wanted; Moroccan wines are expertly chosen and definitely worth investigating. See also La Derrière, below.

Food 7, Service 7, Atmosphere 8

Allard *(left)*

41 rue Saint-André-des-Arts, 6ème
Tel: 01 43 26 48 23
Open: daily, noon–2pm, 7–10.30pm. Closed Sundays and three weeks in August.
French/traditional bistro €80

Beloved of French celebs *and* American tourists, this is an out-and-out classic, serving traditional food (NB that doesn't mean *steak frites*) in the heart of St-Germain. Allard is one of those bistro institutions where nothing much has changed in 75 years: the red banquettes, stained-glass windows and zinc-topped bar are all present and correct, as are the handful of elderly regulars (and waiters) who have been eating/serving duck *aux olives* at Allard since Georges Pompidou's day. Let the bow-tied staff set the pace – they know what they're doing – and take your time over your snails and roast Bresse chicken. The lunch and dinner menus may seen dear, but they're great value for such faultless food. Our top tip: order your *tarte fine aux pommes* when you're ordering your main.

Food 7, Service 8, Atmosphere 7

Apicius *(right)*

20 rue d'Artois, 8ème
Tel: 01 43 80 19 66
Open: noon–2.30pm, 7.30–11pm. Closed Saturdays and Sundays.
French/haute cuisine €150

There's something very Claude Chabrol about Apicius: the sound of gravel crunching beneath your feet as you approach the aristocratic 19th-century mansion; the whiffs of power and corruption that cling to the rich clientele; and the absurdly aristocratic menu. Foie gras comes in two services, €90 for two, rib of beef is served *saignant uniquement*, €110, and even the puddings are called things like 'grand dessert tout caramel', €20. To the right of the entrance and the contemporary bar is a long corridor, off which more or less private rooms are decorated in a timelessly classical style. The regu-

lars are old-school and certainly not impressed by any of it. We are, though, and even more so since we know the building is owned by film-maker Luc Besson, who has his production offices above. Reservations are essential.

Food 8, Service 9, Atmosphere 8

 L'Atelier de *(left)*
Joël Robuchon
5 rue de Montalembert, 7ème
Tel: 01 42 22 56 56
Open: daily, 11.30am–3.30pm,
6.30pm–midnight
French/gourmet **€75**

Surprising but true: here's a glossy, international concept restaurant whose hot status is wholly merited. The big idea is small plates of exquisite, inventive gourmet food, served at the counter of an open kitchen, so you can witness the freshness and the deftness as you dine. The decor is minimal and glossy, with a Japanese bent; the staff are black-clad and the clientele moneyed to at least some degree; to reach contentment via the miniature interpretations of langoustines, frog's legs, scallops, carbonara pasta and calf's liver, a certain abandonment is necessary. Because of the counter arrangement, L'Atelier is best sampled à deux; you can't book, so turning up on the early or late side is wise. Don't miss the warm Chartreuse soufflé.

Food 9, Service 7, Atmosphere 8

Benoît *(top)*
20 rue St-Martin, 4ème
Tel: 01 42 72 25 76

www.alain-ducasse.com
Open: daily, noon–2pm, 7.30–10pm.
Closed last week February.
French/traditional bistro **€90**

Alain Ducasse is in charge here so, as well as everything else, you get to try his signature *savarin au rhum*, served with a choice of rums. Back to the beginning, though: Benoît is a piece of Paris history, a classic bistro founded in 1912, and has been preserved intact, its walls and banquettes the colour of cheese and claret. The menu sticks to tradition, too, featuring pâté en croute, snails, real *cassoulet*, and calf's head; the Ducasse is in the details, such as phenomenally good bread, and *petits fours* served with coffee. It's definitely fancy for a bistro, with prices to match, but there's a nicely accessible lunch menu at €34, which even includes the savarin au rhum.

Food 8, Service 8, Atmosphere 8

Brasserie Lipp *(right)*
151 boulevard Saint-Germain, 6ème
Tel: 01 45 48 53 91
Open: daily, 11.30am–1am
French/brasserie **€60**

There are three legendary cafés in the 6ème, whose memories are truly Proustian, Sartean, Hemingwayesque and so on. The general consensus is that Café Flore and Les Deux Magots are only good for a *demi* during a literary bar crawl, but that Brasserie Lipp is a still-majestic, if touristy landmark. The Art Nouveau tiles, mosaic and mirrors are the real thing, as are the imperious waiters; the menu of

choucroute, herring Bismarck and stuffed pig's trotters is momentously good, and the *millefeuille* is a celebrity in its own right. Talking of A-list, B-list and so on, it's not usual to get a ground-floor table unless you're a somebody; and the usual form is to turn up and wait half an hour for a table.

Food 7, Service 7, Atmosphere 8

Café de l'Homme *(left)*
Musée de l'Homme, 17 place du Trocadéro, 16ème
Tel: 01 44 05 30 15
www.cafedelhomme.com
Open: daily, noon–3pm (11am–4pm Sat–Sun), 7.45–11.30pm;
French/fusion   **€75**

Unique and celebratory, and a complete change from calf's head, this museum restaurant has become a rave among fashion editors, English ex-pats and well-to-do Paris families (plus their dogs, the night we were there). It's all alive with party energy after dark, the mood set by reggae-disco and diners in groups, as well as pairs. The food is great, if verging on steep (clue: you're paying for the view). We can report flawless salmon with *sauce vierge*, great chips, organic *steak tartare* (no capers, though) and a memorably delicious 'deconstructed' lemon tart. Still, it's neither the cooking nor the hangar-like, red-lit dining room, its lights made from tumbling crystals, that you're really here for – the big deal is the full-frontal view of the Eiffel Tower from the terrace, which really does afford a bit of a thrill.

Food 7, Service 7, Atmosphere 8

Le Chateaubriand *(right)*
129 avenue Parmentier, 11ème
Tel: 01 43 57 45 95
Open: noon–2pm, 8–11pm. Closed Sundays, Mondays and August.
Modern French   **€45**

Self-taught Basque chef Iñaki Aizpitarte gives a good name to both culinary deconstruction and strange pairings, with his *steak tartare*, tuna with chorizo, and chocolate custard with Espelette pepper. His modish food, the good-value wine list and Chateabriand's location in prime *bobo* territory have propelled the restaurant's popularity into the stratosphere, with queues at lunchtime and desperation at dinner (those in the know turn up around half nine to wait for a second sitting). The interior has been kept simple and old-fashioned, with bare walls and blackboards listing daily specials. Aizpitarte's menu is short and changes often, according to what's fresh and good. It's almost as hard to get a prime-time spot here as it is at L'Astrance or Guy Savoy – and this is waaaay cooler.

Food 9, Service 7, Atmosphere 8

Chez l'Ami Jean *(bottom)*
27 rue Malar, 7ème
Tel: 01 47 05 86 89
Open: noon–2pm. Closed Sundays, Mondays and in August.
Basque   **€55**

One of those bistros that many an industry insider tips as a favourite, L'Ami Jean is the oldest Basque restaurant in Paris, and a place of contemporary foodie pilgrimage, attracting a true cross-section of diners. It pairs boisterous informality (you might be seated near a table of rugby players or firemen) with superb gourmet food, much of it using ingredients from the southwest: the menu might feature *cochonnaille*, aka great hams from the Camdeborde family (see Le Comptoir du Relais, below), milk-fed lamb from the Pyrénées, foie gras, wild boar and pigeon; whelks, langoustines and seabass are from Brittany. The wine list features distinctive Basque grape varieties, such as tannat from Irouleguy. Do book ahead, even during the week; there's never much of a lull.

Food 8, Service 7, Atmosphere 7

Chez Janou *(top)*
2 rue Roger Verlomme, 3ème
Tel: 01 42 72 28 41
Open: daily, noon–2.30pm, 7.30pm–12.30am
French/Provençal **€45**

Even if you've booked, you may have to wait a while before you're seated at this high-energy, informal bistro but, once you're ensconced with your *moules gratinées à la provencale* and a bottle of Côtes du Rhône, all is happiness. Rich kids and hard-working creatives rub shoulders among the Marcel Pagnol film posters, bits of *brocante*, the odd tub of lavender and antique lamps, generating more and more volume as the night proceeds. It's more than just a Provençal theme: the menu, chalked up on blackboards, features lots of rosemary, *pistou*, spelt and olives, and the wine list is all about the warm south. And, yes, there really are 80 varieties of pastis in the world, and they're all lined up on a shelf at

Chez Janou.

Food 8, Service 7, Atmosphere 9

Chez Omar *(bottom)*
47 rue de Bretagne, 3ème
Tel: 01 42 72 36 26
Open: daily, noon–2.30pm, 7–11.30pm; 7–11.30pm Sun
North African **€40**

Omar was hotly trendy for a while, and still holds its own during Paris Fashion Week. The queues may have diminished, but it's still a buzzing, relaxed place to come for huge, fluffy mounds of correctly made *couscous* and trencherman's portions of roasted meat. The venerably scruffy dining room, with its wooden panelling, matching chairs and paper tablecloths, is full of happy noise, orchestrated charmingly by friendly waiters; on the zinc bar stand fresh flowers (from the market on rue de Bretagne, one of the oldest in Paris). You're not really here for the starters; rather, order a *couscous royale* to share – you get the grain, the veg, and a great platter of lamb, chicken and *merguez* sausages. Puddings include a 'mystery' ice-cream and wonderful pastries from La Bague de Kenza on the rue St-Maur. Chez Omar is great for groups, fine if you're on your own, but not so great for a tête a tête. No credit cards.

Food 6, Service 8, Atmosphere 7

Chez Paul *(top)*

13 rue de Charonne, 11ème
Tel: 01 47 00 34 57
Open: daily, noon–3pm, 7pm–
12.30am; noon–12.30am Sat–Sun
French/bistro **€45**

Let's say you're young and in love, in Paris for the first time. You can't afford Allard and you're not impressed by the new bistronomic cheffery. You want a super-French vibe, and a fleamarket-chic setting so perfect it could almost be a film set? Welcome to Chez Paul on rue de Charonne (not to be confused with its also-good namesake on the rue de Butte aux Cailles). The several small dining rooms are done out with well-worn wooden chairs, junk-shop art and vintage posters and chunky radiators; you get a nice degree of formality for your money, mostly supplied by veteran waiters in white aprons. The menu doesn't stray from French tradition, featuring snails, *crudités*, leek vinaigrette and marrowbone among the two dozen starters, and robust meat and offal dishes for mains. It gets busy, so do book; if you get a walk-in anywhere near 9pm, you're very lucky.

Food 7, Service 8, Atmosphere 7

Le Comptoir du Relais *(left)*

9 carrefour de l'Odéon, 6ème
Tel: 01 44 27 07 97
Open: daily, noon–6pm, 8.30–11pm;
noon–11pm Sat–Sun. Closed part of
August .
French/gastronomic brasserie €65

Hotly promoted by gourmet Parisians and, notably, by chef-patron's Yves Camdeborde's peers within the restaurant industry, Le Comptoir, a bustling St Germain bistro in all but its gastronomic feats, can be a tricky one in terms of securing a table for dinner, even if you mount an all-out telephone assault, weeks in advance. To make life easier, turn up for elevenses of delicious, deboned pig's trotters, or a teatime treat of perfect *pâté en croute*; alternatively, stay at the hotel that houses Camdeborde's dining room, and you'll be in with much more of a shout. The big attraction is the €50 five-course *prix fixe* menu, ideally taken at one of the pavement tables, accompanied by a bottle of rosé. Everything from the charcuterie (ample) to the cheeseboard (delectable), via roasted saddle of lamb with vegetable-filled Basque ravioli and herby jus (incredible), comes together as a very pleasurable picture of where Paris eating is at right now. So keep walking past and trying your luck.

Food 9, Service 8, Atmosphere 9

Le Cristal Room *(right)*

11 place des États-Unis, 16ème
Tel: 01 40 22 11 10
Open: 12.15–2.15pm; 7.30pm–midnight. Closed Sundays
French **€100**

It's hard not to snort with amazement/ amusement at such a palatial (don't mention the 'bling' word) dining room, reached via a literally sparkling staircase inside the Paris HQ of Baccarat, the 250-year-old crystal brand. Actually, laughter isn't inappropriate; they did bring in Philippe Starck, after all, to install pretty pink benches and cushions, exposed brickwork and oversized pieces of furniture among the ornate mouldings. Beneath crystal chandeliers, what else, business regulars and local plutocrats eat rich, playful French cuisine, with lavish resort to lobster, caviar and foie gras a given. Talking of lobsters, Salvador Dalí used to be among the guests at the legendary parties thrown in the building by its former owner, Marie-Laure de Noailles, along with fellow artists Pablo Picasso, Henri Matisse and François Picabia.

Food 7, Service 8, Atmosphere 6

....

Curieux Spaghetti Bar *(top)*
14 rue Saint Merri, 4ème
Tel: 01 42 72 75 97
www.curieuxspag.com
Open: daily, noon–2am (4am Fri/Sat); 11am–2am Sun
Italian   **€40**

Youthful and ultra-relaxed, a gay-boy-staffed pre-club snackery, with the emphasis on yards and yards of spag. Only tangentially Italian, Le Curieux's not aimed at purists but rather provides hot and wholesome fast food: you can go lavish (spaghetti with foie gras or scallops), exotic (wasabi noodles), or off-piste (risotto). Or snort down good-value house wine and share a *plancha italienne* or big bowl of pasta between two or three of you. Since it's open all afternoon, located in prime tourist territory (great for Beaubourg and the Marais in general), there's a broad mix of diners: earlier in the afternoon it's eminently family-friendly; then, post-midnight, the creatures of the night arrive, half of whom barely eat a thing, in spite of free olives and scraps of pizza. The decor is an eyeful of bright,

functional kitsch, with frequently re-vamped wallpaper, rococo chandeliers and high stools; there's an energetic vibe, with customers standing around, on the move, chatting and wolfing down carbs and cocktails with gusto.

Food 6, Service 7, Atmosphere 8

....

Derrière   *(bottom)*
69 rue des Gravilliers, 3ème
Tel: 01 44 61 91 95
Open: daily, noon–2.30pm (4pm Sat/Sun), 8pm–2am
French   **€65**

Formerly a rag-trade workshop, the third piece in Mourad Mazouz's hip and charming Montorgueil triptych is unconventional and hilarious. It opened in autumn 2008, behind (hence the name) 404 restaurant and Andy Wahloo cocktail bar (see Drink), with which it shares the central courtyard. It's a concept bistro, but don't yawn – it's brilliant! It's meant to be like being in someone's house, so there's a 'living room' with a ping pong table and loads of books and CDs, a tatty bedroom up-stairs with tables set up along the edge of the bed, and a smoking room that you enter via a wardrobe, à la Narnia. It's great fun, completely irreverent and, perhaps surprisingly, the food is terrific: you might eat artichokes with Espelette pepper jam, grilled turbot with creamy polenta, and *millefeuille* with vanilla custard. Watch out for ping pong balls in your tiramisu!

Food 8, Service 7, Atmosphere 9

eat...

Drouant (left)
18 rue Gaillon, 2ème
Tel: 01 42 65 15 16 www.drouant.com
Open: daily, noon–2.30pm,
7pm–midnight
French/smart brasserie   **€80**

Another grand old-timer, this one a magnificent, masculine brasserie dating from 1880, Drouant hasn't been allowed to become a dusty relic, thanks to the intervention of Alsatian superchef Antoine Westermann, who also runs Mon Vieil Ami on the Ile St Louis. He does playful things to classical cuisine, especially with the starters and puddings, which often come as multiple takes on one idea, be it Asian beef salad or leek vinaigrette. The interior has been sleekly revamped in golden-yellow tones, with glossy black lamps; the names inscribed around the façade are all past winners of the Goncourt Prize, whose judges have been deliberating at Drouant for decades. It's very establishment, very upscale, and very Paris.

Food 8, Service 9, Atmosphere 7

L'Ecailler du Bistrot (bottom)
20–22 rue Paul Bert, 11ème
Tel: 01 43 72 76 77
Open: noon–2.30pm, 7.30–11pm.
Closed Sundays and Mondays.
French/seafood   **€55**

Attached by marriage to the famed Bistrot Paul Bert next-door (owner Gwenaëlle Cadoret is married to Bernard Auboyneau of BPB), this seafood brasserie does what it does very well – and that is seafood. Oysters from Brittany and Normandy (Cadoret

is the daughter of a Breton *huitrier*) are served by the dozen, nine or six, priced according to size, and accompanied by sourdough bread and two kinds of fine butter. The seafood platter for two comes on ice, swathed in seaweed and all of it fresh, oceanic and expertly conveyed from sea to plate: clams, winkles, shrimps, bigger, pinker shrimps, spider crab and more oysters. Just add Muscadet. Puddings are amazing, especially the fondant au chocolat, which comes with *crème anglaise* and goes in a trice. The interior is chipper and nautical, with lots of wood, blues and yellows.

Food 8, Service 8, Atmosphere 9

La Fidelité (right)
4 rue de la Fidelité, 10ème
Tel: 01 47 70 19 34
Open: noon–3pm, 7–11pm. Closed
Saturdays and Sundays.
French/modern brasserie   **€50**

Brand-new when we visited, this self-proclaimed 'modern brasserie' is owned by the nightlife promoters known as La Clique, who have become quasi-celebrities with the success of their clubs Paris, Paris, Le Baron and Le Régine (see Party). But never mind the hype, the models, the pedigree – is it any good? In terms of cuisine, style and good times, definitely yes, though the service is glacially slow; we ate eggy, substantial mackerel tartare, tender beef cheek with *sauce vierge*, and simple, lovely turbot with endives. The dining room is impressively big and rigorously undesigned. There's no art, just red banquettes, white tablecloths and fresh flowers. It'll be interesting to see how it goes here once the pretty young things have moved on. If you ask us, La Fidelité ought to be a hit on the strength of its deconstructed *mille-feuille* alone.

Food 7, Service 6, Atmosphere 7

 Fish La Boissonnerie *(left)*
69 rue de Seine, 6ème
Tel: 01 43 54 34 69
Open: 12.30–3pm, 7–10.45pm.
Closed Mondays.
Wine bar/seafood bistro   €50

This punning St Germain bistro used to be a fishmongers, and now concentrates on fish (as distinct from seafood) and regional wines. It has a homely appeal, with tiled floors, old photographs hung on ancient stone walls and a zinc bar. The comfortable, Mediterranean vibe continues on the menu, where you might see smoked salmon linguini with a yellow-pepper sauce, or seabass served with piperade; the wine list features the *cepages*, ie: the grape varieties, which pleases oenophiles no end. The regulars are a well-heeled locals, older, smarter and with more expensive tans than the young species who congregate on Rue de Buci, just down the road. The owners are from New Zealand, and also run the wine shop called La Dernière Goutte, nearby at 6 rue de Bourbon le Château, which does tastings some weekends.

Food 8, Service 8, Atmosphere 7

 La Fontaine de Mars *(right)*
129 rue Saint-Dominique, 7ème

Tel: 01 47 05 46 44
Open: daily, noon–3pm, 7.30–11pm
French/bistro   €75

There's a south-western bias at La Fontaine de Mars, which of course doesn't complicate at all its traditional bistro regime: waiters career gracefully to and fro across the tiled floor, conveying trencherman portions of black pudding with apples, *cassoulet* and *baba au rhum*; diners take their time to talk and laugh, especially in summer, when a dozen or so tables are set out in the square, overlooking the eponymous statuary; and wine flows as per usual in such a pleasure-focused establishment. The decorative tropes of the bistro are all in order: the smart banquettes, the brass rails, the mirrors, the menu chalked up on a blackboard. Note that though the red farmhouse tablecloths may be rustic, the pricing definitely isn't; this humble Gascon kitchen is hard by the Quai Branly and the Eiffel Tower. Do book in advance and try to arrange to be ravenous, rather than merely hungry.

Food 7, Service 7, Atmosphere 8

Le Fumoir *(bottom)*
6 rue de l'Amiral-de-Coligny, 1er
Tel: 01 42 92 00 24 www.lefumoir.com
Open: daily, 11am–2am
French   €50

Where, oh where to find refreshment when you've just staggered out of the Louvre? The correct answer is Le Fumoir, famous for its Sunday brunch, but just as much of a pleasure midweek for elevenses, a pot of premium tea or

the apéritif. The casually chic crowd encompasses every generation, from children to matrons in Chanel flats, and there's ample room in a series of rooms and on the terrace (indoors is nicer, though). The main bar has a slightly scuffed colonial appeal, with unvarnished wooden floors and ceiling fans, whirring in harmony with jazz and cocktails being shaken; there's more of a restaurant feel in the rear rooms, where you can order from a sophisticated brasserie menu. This is also among our favourite places to come alone with a notebook, novel or the laptop.

Food 7, Service 8, Atmosphere 7

La Gazzetta *(top)*
9 rue de Cotte, 12ème
Tel: 01 43 47 47 05
Open: 11.30pm–3pm, 6.30pm–1am.
Closed Mondays.
French/modern bistro   **€55**

Residents of the Bastille area are delighted with this neighbourhood bistro, which offers something a little different, thanks to the Swedish chef's melding of influences from all over France with Scandinavian herbs and potato dishes. The thirtysomething regulars approve of the streamlined Art Deco stylings, the dim lighting and the breadth of the short wine list, which visits the Baleares, Corsica, Italy and Spain, even Lebanon. La Gazzetta is low on formality and high on democratic cool; in its quiet way, it's one of the restaurants revolutionising French dining. The lunch *formule* at €16 is a 'bistronomic' bargain, offering tapas-sized appetisers, as well as a starter and a main; but the real action's at dinner; come with a group, so you can try one another's petit pois and ricotta ravioli, and roast pigeon with smoked aubergine and raw and cooked cauliflower.

Food 7, Service 7, Atmosphere 7

Georges *(bottom)*
6th Floor, Centre Pompidou,
rue Rambuteau, 4ème
Tel: 01 44 78 47 99
Open: noon–1am. Closed Tuesdays.
French/fusion   **€60**

Fancy poncy places like Georges rule, in a way that rustic-chic bistros can't. That is because the sexy staff, the futuretastic design, the top-of-the-world location and, of course, the gastronomic concept (check out the cinematic titles of the good but not sensational Asian-fusion food) are not of this world. Get ready for slight aloofness from the waiters as you ascend via the transparent tubes, then hold your own among the glossy pods, and you'll have a terrific time, consuming California rolls, tuna tartare, steak and cocktails. Finally, don't approach the restaurant from the front of the Pompidou Centre (the way in is round the other side). In fact, don't approach it in the dark on an empty stomach unless you kind of know where you're going – falling over and hurting your knee among the Beaubourg's health-and-safety-flouting architectural trappings is not glamorous.

Food 7, Service 6, Atmosphere 8

eat...

Higuma *(top)*
32 bis rue Sainte-Anne, 1er
Tel: 01 47 03 38 59
Open: daily, 11.30am–10pm
Japanese   **€15**

Plain looks, precious few concessions to anything resembling service, and daily queues at lunchtime – yet this noodle canteen comes avidly recommended. You won't wait long, since the brow-mopping, wok-jerking chefs do their thing at lightning speed, plus there are three rooms to accommodate the peaktime horde of hungry workers – it'll be your go before you can say 'where are my dumplings?' It's noisy and steamy and makes a nice, clean change from steak, *saucisson* and St Marcellin; whether you ask for meat, seafood or vegetables, you ought to walk away feeling wholesome and energised. There are several similarly styled pitstops on the same drag, but this is the top choice for an appetite-slaying bowl of tip-top-value sustenance.

Food 8, Service 6, Atmosphere 6

Hôtel du Nord *(middle)*
102 quai de Jemmapes, 10ème
Tel: 01 40 40 78 78
www.hoteldunord.org
Open: daily, 10am–2am. Food served noon–2.30pm; 8–11.30pm.
Fusion   **€45**

Although Hôtel du Nord is no longer a hotel, the sign on the façade is listed, because Eugène Dabit's novel of the same name, turned into a legendary film by Marcel Carné in the 1930s, is set here. A few years back, the premises were taken over by young nightlife entrepreneurs, and became a relaxed restaurant serving a fusion of French, Spanish and Asian food. At entrance level: white tiled walls, black and white floors, a zinc bar, bare tables and bentwood chairs. The raised restaurant area at the back is cosier, with tablecloths, flowers and shelves of books; there are sexy/cool 20th-century photographs dotted around the walls throughout. The food is simple and light and less outré than 'fusion' suggests, with the *formule midi* very good value at €13.50 for two courses. By night, summer weather brings young professionals out to socialise at a handful of tables overlooking the canal. The owners' latest trick, over on the swanky Right Bank, is Le ChaCha (see Party).

Food 7, Service 7, Atmosphere 8

Le Jules Verne *(bottom)*
2nd level, Pilier Sud, Tour Eiffel, 7ème
Tel: 01 45 55 61 44
Open: daily, 12.15–1.30pm; 7.15–9.30pm
French/haute cuisine   **€175**

Expect stratospheric everything when you dine on Alain Ducasse's recently revamped pie in the sky: fabulous food, sublime design, views of Paris from 125 metres up the Iron Lady's legs, and the pleasure of increasing your personal status by getting a reservation (book ahead, seriously). On the menu are silken adaptations of beef tournedos with duck foie gras, turbot with champagne sauce, pink grapefruit

soufflé and an Eiffel-inspired praline nut (served without a bolt). The front-of-house staff – especially the team of master sommeliers – are as impeccable as you'd hope from Ducasse; and the superchef's preference for gorgeous, craftsman-produced table settings has never been more appropriate than in this symbolic dining room. Patrick Jouin, who also designed Ducasse's restaurants at the Dorchester and the Plaza Athenée, has created a sumptuous eyrie, with carbon-fibre seating engineered by the Pininfarina studio.

Food 9, Service 9, Atmosphere 8

Market *(top)*
15 avenue Matignon, 8ème
Tel: 01 56 43 40 90
Open: daily, noon–3pm (4.30pm Sat/Sun), 7–11.30pm
Fusion **€80**

There's something of the late 1990s about Market, which makes it perfect when you're not after anything too thrustingly youthful and trendy. If you're a fan of Jean-Georges Vongerichten's New York restaurants, you'll be right at home with the chilled soundtrack and blond-toned, minimal decor. There are dishes weird and wonderful on the Asian fusion menu, such as a pizza with raw tuna and wasabi cream; you can't go wrong with the Black Plate starter of spring rolls, dumplings, sushi and grilled quail, each with its own sauce, to share between two. A short, up-to-date cocktail list offers kumquat mojitos and cucumber martinis. The weekend brunch menu offers both eggs Benedict and papaya salad with squid and cashew nuts; and you're only a short walk from the Champs Elysées and Rue St-Honoré.

Food 8, Service 7, Atmosphere 7

eat...

La Mascotte *(middle)*
52 rue des Abbesses, 18ème
Tel: 01 46 06 28 15
Open: daily, noon–3pm, 7pm–midnight; noon–midnight Sat/Sun
French/traditional brasserie **€40**

Even some of the most jaded Parisians *de souche* find themselves weak with nostalgia at the mention of La Mascotte, so authentic is its old-school atmos, and so appealing are its fittings and fixtures – including the waiters. For those after an unpretentious feed-up with a side order of unremarked-upon eccentricity (plus live accordion tunes on Sundays), it's the tops. Nothing about the Art Deco dining room has been significantly updated since time immemorial, from oyster stand to lobster tank. The food is even-tempered brasserie fare; you can't go far wrong if you stick to aforementioned Atlantic bivalves, crustacea and a nice *Pouilly Fumé*. Puddings tend to be doused in strong liquor, even sometimes the Berthillon ices. A relic to relish.

Food 7, Service 6, Atmosphere 8

Le Meurice *(bottom)*
Hotel Meurice, 228 rue de Rivoli, 1er
Tel: 01 44 58 10 10
www.lemeurice.com
Open: 7am–10am, 12.30–2pm, 7.30–10.30pm. Closed Saturday, Sundays and throughout August
Haute cuisine **€250**

Lord, isn't Paris full of amazing, expensive restaurants? Can there be a top of the tops? We couldn't eat at all of them – not even in the name of hedonism – but we did ask many Parisian restaurateurs and rich foodies where to go in order to spend hundreds of euros and eat like a Holy Roman Emperor, and here's where we ended up. Yannick Alléno's restaurant at Le Meurice (see Sleep) is one of some dozen establishments in Paris to carry three Michelin stars; what makes it extra-special is the most beautiful dining room in Paris, all silvery light, fine-veined marble and angels on the ceiling. The food is opulent but not frivolous: Alléno's style is subtle, aromatic and exact. Each dish is ceremoniously introduced by a waiter of the correct rank for that particular course. A recent tasting menu featured crab meat in squid cannelloni served with pink grapefruit and seaweed chutney and almond ice-cream; and larded fillet of beef marinated with seaweed jam. As one of our correspondents declares: 'It always delivers.'

Food 9, Service 9, Atmosphere 9

Le Miroir *(top)*
94 rue des Martyrs, 18ème
Tel: 01 46 06 50 73
Open: noon–2pm, 7–10pm;
noon–2pm Sun. Closed Monday and all of August.
French/modern bistro   **€45**

A welcome newcomer to Montmartre, near the top of rue des Martyrs, Le Miroir looks and feels fairly old-school, with factory-style lamps, red leather banquettes and bare wooden tables with heavy iron bases. The young kitchen team, however, have some impressive experience behind them (not least at the Alain Ducasse bistro Au Lyonnais), so expect new-style classics such as a plate of *cochonnailles* – pâté, sausage and trotter with onion jam – and vanilla *petits pots de crème* with home-made biscuits. The madeleines served with coffee are a nice little tribute to Ducasse. A great place to prolong the last shreds of pleasure if you're leaving town via the Gare du Nord (don't forget to leave time to pick up some macaroons at boulangerie Arnaud Delmontel at number 39).

Food 8, Service 7, Atmosphere 7

Pavillon Ledoyen *(bottom)*
1 avenue Dutuit, 8ème
Tel: 01 53 05 10 01
Open: 12.30pm–2.30pm, 8–9.45pm.
Closed Saturdays, Sundays and Monday lunch, and August.
French/haute cuisine   **€200**

Proudly presented at well-spaced, white-draped tables in a palatial Second Empire dining room, an historic Champs Elysées site where Napoleon Bonaparte famously dined with Josephine, Christian Le Squer's extraordinary food is a major modern thrill. It is at the odder end of experimental, with even the amazing bread selection including squid-ink prawn rolls. Playful *amuse-gueules* such as liquid-centred foie gras croquettes and beetroot macaroons, and pre-dessert teasers of tiny skewered marshmallows and toffee apples filled with Granny Smith sorbet give an idea of the deftness and brilliance of the chefs. You might eat veal with herb and rocket cannelloni or game terrine with gold-leafed savoury jelly, then turbot served with truffled Ratte potatoes, followed by the most sublime *millefeuille* or passionfruit and pineapple soufflé. The service is of the 'safety in numbers' school, with extras in every scene. At €88, the set lunch menu is outstanding value for three-Michelin-star food.

Food 9, Service 7, Atmosphere 7

Le Petit Marché *(left)*
9 rue de Béarn, 4ème
Tel: 01 42 72 06 67
Open: daily, noon–3pm (4pm Sat–Sun), 7.45pm–midnight
French/bistro **€50**

This assured Marais bistro is just off Place des Vosges, the oldest square in Paris, and has a businesslike charm. It's small, verging on cramped, with a beamed ceiling, and a corner decorated with portraits of various enigmatic women; the service can be a bit clunky, yet it's packed out every lunchtime with art dealers and lawyers, who know a good-value thing when they find it. The little open kitchen turns out contemporary bistro food with Asian touches, such as pollock with dill-scented beurre blanc, or raw tuna with Thai sauce. Agreeably untouristy, given the location.

Food 7, Service 6, Atmosphere 7

Au Pied de Fouet *(right)*
45 rue de Babylone, 7ème
Tel: 01 47 05 12 27
Open: noon–2.30pm, 7–11pm.
Closed Sundays.

French/bistro **€40**

Very old and very tiny, Au Pied de Fouet packs a handful of tables onto each of its no-frills floors and feeds its faithful clientele with unpretentious French cuisine: *blanquette de veau* or *tripoux*, washed down with decent wine. Authentically enough, the chef-patron is from the Auvergne, where the originators of the city's first bistros were from. Regulars have their own numbered napkins, stored in the *meuble à serviettes*; all comers are seated cheek-by-jowl, in front of checked tablecloths and gleaming wine glasses. There's now a second location, on rue St-Benoît in the 6ème.

Food 7, Service 7, Atmosphere 8

Le Réfectoire *(bottom)*
80 boulevard Richard Lenoir, 11ème
Tel: 01 48 06 74 85
www.lerefectoire.com
Open: daily, noon–2.30pm, 8–11.30pm
French **€35**

Previously dabbling in fusion cuisine, Le Réfectoire has dropped the experimental airs and settled into a more convincing incarnation as a trendy but friendly neighbourhood gem, run with a lot of care by a bunch of terribly nice boys. The food is French but not rustic: most of its clientele come for a good *steak tartare* or *pavé de boeuf* and a bottle of Vacqueyras. The menu, formatted variously for brunch, lunch or dinner, also offers big, delicious salads, a charcuterie platter and an unbelievably good *petit pot au lait*. The (graphic) design is fun and gives the place its own

energetic identity; there's a perspex floor and an old reel-to-reel in the loo, and oversized molecular models hanging from the ceiling (bit of a schoolroom theme going on). The value for money is remarkable, and there's a happy vibe among the clientele of locals, young families and a few anglais.

Food 8, Service 9, Atmosphere 7

Le Rousseau *(left)*
45 rue du Cherche-Midi, 6ème
Tel: 01 42 22 51 07
Open: 8am–midnight. Closed Sundays and part of August
French/brasserie €60

Its many regulars – advertising execs, well-to-do artists, fashion-retail bods – keep this family business abustle. There's nothing ground-breaking or trendy to report, just good bistro food, with a Landaise/Basquaise slant, so you might find squid with chorizo or *magret de canard* on the lunch menu. By night, the bistro becomes a restaurant, and pristine white tablecloths are put into service; it's all very civilised, without straying from its neighbourhood status. The decor is warm-toned, a bit theatrical, and features ceramics arranged on oak shelves, crushed-velvet upholstery for the chairs, and a few volumes by some Jean-Jacques Rousseau character – who shares his *nom de famille* with the couple who run the restaurant. There's a sister premises along the street at number 72, called L'Horloge.

Food 7, Service 8, Atmosphere 6

Le Timbre *(right)*
3 rue Sainte-Beuve, 6ème
Tel: 01 45 49 10 40
Open: noon–2pm, 7–10.30pm. Closed Sundays and Monday lunch, first two weeks August
French €40

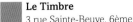

Timbre as in postage stamp, size of a… In his weeny open kitchen, Mancunian chef-patron Chris Wright demonstrates what you can do with skill and simplicity, winning over his adopted city in spite of his self-taught status. Wright's weekly-changing menu is dictated by what's fresh at market, so you might start with ham-wrapped calamari or caramelised onion and anchovy tart, then choose between cod with tarragon purée and pan-fried pork with red onions. Le Timbre's fabulous signature *millefeuille* never comes off the menu; English Cheddar and Stilton from Neal's Yard Dairy are another fixture. There are just 24 covers, so call in advance (it's often Wright who picks up the phone), and glow with pride if you're from Lancashire.

Food 9, Service 8, Atmosphere 8

Le Train Bleu *(bottom)*
Gare de Lyon,
place Louis Armand, 12ème
Tel: 01 43 43 09 06
Open: daily, 11.30am–3pm, 7–11pm
French €90

Very beautiful, ornate and unique, with its 40 antique paintings, each depicting a scene from a location somewhere on the splendid 1900s rail network, Le Train Bleu is, at present, something of a relic. The brasserie food is good, if expensive; the service absolutely charming; and the location unbeatable. Alas, it lacks only a glamorous clientele and buzzing atmosphere; hopefully this ultra-romantic dining room will regain its place among the greats soon, rather than chugging along charmingly. Having said all this, we're rather partial to its faded beauty. Tear off your jeans and Converse, get a little retro, and climb aboard for lobster salad, *Lyon saucission* with warm Ratte potato salad, then veal chop with lasagne or classic breaded pig's trotters. This being a train station, it's an ideal place for heavy relationship conversations, even tears, so long as everything's OK again in time for the booze-soaked rum baba.

Food 7, Service 7, Atmosphere 6

Urbane *(top)*
12 rue Arthur Groussier, 10ème
Tel: 01 42 40 74 75
Open: 12.30pm–3pm; 7.30–11pm.
Closed Mondays.
French/modern bistro **€50**

Everything about Urbane feels like fresh thinking, from the 'nice and quiet' DJs who play vinyl in the little dining room at weekends to the Polaroid art and, definitely, the brilliant value, deceptively skilful food. Lettuce soup tastes exactly right for late spring, bream comes precisely cooked, with mash and beetroot purée, and juicy *pavé* rump steak with grilled polenta is a big hit, flying out of the kitchen. Neat details abound, such as the water that arrives unbidden in a clear, wine-bottle-shaped decanter, the short, idiosyncratic wine list, and great bread.

The clientele look like gentle, academic-leaning professionals; the front-of-house staff is composed entirely of Audrey, the chef's wife, who is run off her feet but clearly enthused about the success of their ambitious local.

Food 8, Service 7, Atmosphere 7

Ze Kitchen Galerie *(bottom)*
4 rue Grands Augustins, 6ème
Tel: 01 44 32 00 32
Open: 12.15–2.15pm, 7.15pm–10.45pm.Closed Saturday lunch and Sundays.
French **€50**

You could be forgiven for thinking 'fusion' when you see the ingredients with which ZKG's William Ledeuil is making his name. He matches burrata cheese with galangal, likes to marinate fish and seafood and serve it with ginger or citrus dressing, and accompanies grilled pigeon with teriyaki jus. Yet this is, he says, contemporary French cuisine, it's just that incorporating Eastern influences is his thing. The restaurant, a few steps from both the Seine and the social bar-hop of Rue de Buci, is cleanly designed, with lots of colour and nothing retro or flouncy – pretty much like the food. Puddings are fruity and globetrotting: roasted Thai mango with coconut, vanilla and passionfruit ice-cream; or white chocolate and wasabi ice-cream with pistachio and strawberry sauce. Much talked-about, and with good reason. As for ze name, ze walls are covered in ze modern art.

Food 9, Service 8, Atmosphere 8

Lè Bar

drink...

The mainstay of traditional bar culture in Paris is anything but a simple boozer. Your classic *tabac-café*, open from early breakfast time till 2am, is likely to serve breakfast, lunch and dinner, and sell lottery tickets and stamps, as well as doling out coffee all day, every day. To the British observer, it's equally reminiscent of a local pub and the village post office. Walk into one early in the morning, and you'll encounter workers propping up the traditional zinc-topped bar, sipping their first espresso of the day (the standard coffee, unless stated otherwise). As the day wears on, drinks are served, at different prices, according to where you stand or sit. For economy-class imbibing, stand at the bar; the most expensive place to drink is at a table on the terrace.

Not all trad bars are *café-tabacs*, of course and, especially in the teeming metropolis, though one bar might look very much like another, they can differ wildly in term of character. Clientele and location – and the age and preference of the owner – will determine whether a given venue feels like a local hub, such as Le Baron Rouge, near the Gare de Lyon; a trendy hang-out, like retro Marais gem La Perle; or both (La Chope du Château Rouge, Le Bar du Marché on Rue Buci). Actual bars, unlike cafés, open around 6pm, and usually see their last customer out any time between 2am and 4am. Most bars play their music loud (Dédé la Frite): some will have DJs every day, others only at weekends. Some feature live bands (Alimentation Générale) and others feel more like clubs (Ice Kube, La Mezzanine de l'Alcazar).

The hipper a bar gets, the less likely you are to be provided with anything like the substantial snackage – plates of charcuterie, omelettes, *croque monsieurs* – offered

Le Baron Rouge

in the average, unreconstructed café. But, whether you find yourself in a Formica-clad relic or a gilded hotel lobby, you'll never have to grin and bear inferior wine. This, along with the pleasure of being able to go out for a coffee without having to segregate yourself from the fun people, is one of the great things about drinking in Paris. At pretty much any bar you like, the cheapest plonk will be better than the wine you can expect in the average UK or US pub or bar. And the unlikeliest places are wine specialists, from authentically vintage Le Rubis on the rue du Marché Saint-Honoré, to homely, shabby-chic Café La Fusée near the Centre Pompidou.

Away from internationally inclined venues, there's no cocktail tradition in wine-loving, brandy-gulping France, though the young knights behind Experimental Cocktail Club are having a great success with their toney, New York-style hang-outs. Rare is the high-end bar that stands on its own; these are more likely to belong a restaurant or hotel, such as the bars at Plaza Athenée, Pershing Hall and Kong. The bars at Hotel Amour, Murano Urban Resort and Le Meurice are all fun and fashionable right now, in very different ways (see Sleep).

To guarantee a good bar crawl, avoid the rue de Lappe (though you should see it to believe it), home to the city's highest concentration of watering holes – every one of them themed and tacky. For a higher class of dive, we recommend the rue Montmartre, the Marais or the rue de Buci in St-Germain-des-Prés. For a serious bender, though, you can't beat the Oberkampf area; the streets to head for are Oberkampf, Jean-Pierre Timbaud and Saint-Maur.

L'Alimentation Générale *(top)*
64 rue Jean-Pierre Timbaud, 11ème
Tel: 01 43 55 42 50
www.alimentation-generale.net
Open: 5pm–2am (5am Fri–Sat).
Closed Mondays and Tuesdays.

There's a roots/world bias, musically, at this shabby-cool dancehall with a young local clientele and a long bar, where you can order not only bottled beer, wine and fruity cocktails but also a nice hot chocolate, and tapas-style bar food to eat with friends or à deux if you're dating a cute indie boy or girl. As the name (grocer's shop, basically) suggests, it's all very inclusive and Oberkampfy, with 'expect the unexpected' programming that includes art exhibitions, film screenings and, at least once, a puppet show, as well as late-night dance parties. The live-music offering – raï, Afrobeat, hip-hip, Parisians' beloved electro DJ sets – is the mainstay, regularly transforming the room into a sweaty musical mess, but quiet nights here have their charm, too, when there's more room to sit and chat among the kitschy junk-shop tat.

Andy Wahloo *(bottom)*
69 rue des Gravilliers, 3ème
Tel: 01 42 71 20 38
Open: 6pm–2am. Closed Sundays and Mondays.

A simple, squareish room plus a little courtyard at the rear, shared with Mourad 'Momo' Mazouz's other two Paris babies, restaurants 404 and Derrière (see Eat), Andy Wahloo – it sounds like 'I have nothing' in Arabic – is relaxed, hip and easy to love. The look is co-

lourful and (very) cheerful, with street signs and cooking-oil barrels recycled as tables and stools, and bright packaging displayed as kitsch art, next to film posters and tourism ads. Imagine an African street market serving ace mojitos and playing Curtis Mayfield, and you're there. It's still buzzing, eight years after opening; you'll be lucky to find a place on the cushion-strewn Moroccan bench seating after 9pm. Great cocktails aside, refreshments include north African wines and mint tea, and there are *tartines* and charcuterie to snack on, supplied by the bar's sister restaurants.

L'Assignat *(right)*
7 rue Guénégaud, 6ème
Tel: 01 43 54 87 68
Open: daily, 9.30am until the last person leaves

The jukebox promises, without a shred of irony, the *Dallas* theme, 'The Final Countdown' by Europe, Boney M and Serge Gainsbourg – what more could you need? Well, inexpensive coffee, table football, curmudgeonly family owners (secretly really nice, you can tell) and good plain food, such as sausage and lentils, burgers or steak tartare are what you get. The name is a reference to a sort of bond issued during the French Revolution, when the government went bankrupt, and the fag-ash-Lil walls are decorated with images of coins and bank notes; the Musée de la Monnaie de Paris, i.e.: the city mint, is opposite. It's a great place to come for a quiet *citron pressé* and a slice of real old Paris, in the company of students from the nearby Ecole des Beaux-Arts.

drink…

Le Bar *(top)*
Le Plaza Athénée, 25 avenue Montaigne, 8ème
Tel: 01 53 67 66 00
www.plaza-athenee-paris.com
Open: daily, 6pm–2am

A successful attempt at coolness from a top-dollar hotel (see Sleep), whose restaurants and *salon de thé* (see Snack) are favourites among the powerful and the international. A younger, slightly less moneyed clientele spend their evenings at Le Bar, ordering champagne cocktails and jelly shots from a 'digital' drinks menu. One end of the nobly proportioned room is dominated by a long, glowing, sculpted-glass bar; high tables and their perches are lit by low-hanging blue chandeliers. The warmer-feeling half has leather club chairs, oversized classical paintings and a video fireplace. When it first opened, turning up on spec to Le Bar was a risky business; now the fuss has died down, it's still a classy place to take the weight off your Manolos.

Le Bar du Marché *(middle)*
75 rue de Seine, 6ème (on the corner with Rue Buci)
Tel: 01 43 26 55 15
Open: daily, 8am–2am

Of all the watering holes on Rue de Buci – a veritable gift to the Paris pub crawler – the Bar de Marché (there's a little open-air market here daily) is 'the one'. The people-watching is supreme, the waiters' funny uniform of dungarees and beret is… funny, and = good times are guaranteed, whether that's a prolonged *café crème* on the terrace on a Saturday morning or a midwinter, midnight chat on one of the racing-car red banquettes in the back room. The classic café trappings of mirrors, antique light fittings, brass-topped bar and vintage film posters have been jazzed up amusingly with a pink neon light over the bar and a disco ball. N.B.: the more frantic you are to get the waiter's attention, the longer you'll wait – it's just one of those places.

BarOurcq *(bottom)*
68 quai de la Loire, 19ème
Tel: 01 42 40 12 26
Open: 3pm–midnight (2am Fri/Sat, 10ish Sun). Closed Mondays and Tuesdays.

A bar that's very much about relaxing, with tangential possibilities for drinking, playing pétanque, flirting, sunbathing and meeting new friends, BarOurcq is a summertime favourite for canalside beers and caipirinha shots. It's easy to find, with its turquoise exterior and corner site; walk up the canal from the Marais towards Parc de la Villette, and you'll come across it just as you're getting really thirsty… DJ sets at 6pm and 10pm on Fridays and Saturdays inject energy, though really this is a chilled-out venue, somewhere to sink into an old sofa with a drink or chat outdoors until closing time. It goes into hibernation in winter, emerging only at weekends until the chilly months are over, so ring to check times.

drink…

Le Baron Rouge *(top)*

1 rue Théophile-Roussel, 12ème

Tel: 01 43 43 14 32

Open: 10am–2pm, 5–10pm
Tues–Thurs; 10am–10pm Fri–Sat;
10am–4pm Sun. Closed Mondays.

A lovely local *bar à vin* by the Rue de Cotte, a short walk from the Gare de Lyon, with café furniture, tiled floor and huge wooden casks serving a dual functional/decorative role. Bantering regulars cluster by the corner of the bar, so that it's hard to to tell them apart from the staff. A salt-of-the-earth, pubby vibe reigns, and it's a friendly, low-key place to come solo; you're never alone at the Baron Rouge (that's what it said on the awning last time we looked; sometimes it's known as the Baron Bouge). Oysters, *rillettes de la mer* and cheese or charcuterie platters are prepared out the back, so you can drop in for a glass of Burgundy and a slice of ham, or half a dozen Atlantic oysters and a glass of Chablis. During the day, there's often a happy little crowd on the pavement – the perfect advert for a very nice bar.

Le Brébant *(left)*

32 boulevard Poissonnière, 9th

Tel: 01 47 70 01 02

Open: daily, 7.30am–6am

A zinc bar as long as a bendy bus, which serves connoisseurs' bottled beers and expertly concocted cocktails: mojitos, daiquiris and some lesser-known humdingers made with premium booze such as Bombay Sapphire or Stolichnaya. The split-level interior doesn't look like much, but up-to-the-minute styling is irrelevant to the crowds of party people who appreciate Le Brébant's excellent opening times – it's a favourite post-clubbing pitstop for a club sandwich – and its even more thoughtful Happy Hour, every day between 7pm and 9pm when all drinks, including those mojito royales, are half price. The mishmash of coloured steel chairs, red banquettes, wrought iron curlicues and bare lightbulbs is somewhat naff; the dance music on the sound system is spot-on for the Grands Boulevards locale, near Social Club and Rex (see Party).

Café Charbon *(right)*

109 rue Oberkampf, 11ème

Tel: 01 43 57 55 13

Open: daily, 9am–2am (4am Thurs–Sat)

Credited with kickstarting the nightlife scene that's now synonymous with Oberkampf, Café Charbon is still the first place we'd recommend for a drink on that strip. If the magnificently restored interior is all high ceilings, Belle Epoque murals, mirrors and vintage light fittings, the typical regular is more of a Joey Ramone character, even more so by night, when the bar acts as warm-up zone for the sister club and music venue Nouveau Casino (see Live Music). During the day, you could bring your parents – it's not intimidatingly trendy, and the sense of history gives it across-the-board appeal. If your parents are ageing punks, so much the better. Staff are friendly and professional, and the clientele are blessedly unpretentious. Wines of the month, cocktail specials and brunch dishes are suggested on blackboards propped here and there.

Café Chic *(top)*

126 rue du Faubourg-Saint-Honoré, 8ème
Tel: 01 45 63 69 69
Open: daily, 8am–5am
(4am Sun–Tues)

There's something of the racing driver or Premier League soccer player about Café Chic, a louche, naughty-looking regulars' bar in a toney part of town – although plenty of its clientele are lawyers and financiers. Bling is alive and well here, in the form of gold lamp bases moulded to resemble machine guns, shocking-pink ceilings and black walls. It's a late-night cocktail bar for an older, richer crowd, serving classic cocktails at €14 a pop, and tapas-style food (available till 3am); upstairs is a big lounge, very 1980s Manhattan, with white leather armchairs, black slatted blinds and bamboo plants. The music policy is brilliant, from easy-going soul to Charles Aznavour, Britney, Madonna; DJs are on most nights. Definitely a hedonist's den, perhaps not for everyone (that means you, *Wallpaper** readers) but stacks of fun.

Café La Fusée *(left)*

168 rue Saint-Martin, 3ème
Tel: 01 42 76 93 99
Open: daily, 10am–2am

Simple, friendly and immensely likable, Café la Fusée is a true haven among the hit-and-miss bars of the touristy Beaubourg area, and a good resort near the Pompidou Centre. In fine weather, the whole place is open onto the street, with plenty of pavement tables and mismatched chairs beneath a cheerful red and white striped awning. Inside, embellishments are restricted to shelves of knackered books, posters of past exhibitions at the Pompidou Centre, and a promising-looking cabinet of wine. Soups, salads and *croque monsieurs* are served till 4pm, with cheese and ham platters available later on. There's live music on Sundays (jazz, gypsy, Brazilian), which draws a big, sociable crowd.

Le China *(right)*

50 rue de Charenton, 12ème
Tel: 01 43 46 08 09
Open: daily, 8am–2am

Re-opened in 2008 under new ownership, but barely changed, the former China Club is still a civilised, sexy den, miraculously neither seedy nor flashy. It's a straight-up tribute to old Shanghai, with Chinese red walls, chequerboard flooring and Art Deco wall sconces in the main bar, bamboo plants and carved dark-wood screens in the upstairs restaurant, and colonial-style blinds and club chairs in the former smoking room. There's plenty of room, the cocktails are good, and graceful service adds to the escapist atmosphere, though the decor alone should transport you far, far from Opéra Bastille. We can't recommend the restaurant or the downstairs salon *dansant* as avidly as the bar. Also, hold the Susie Wong dress unless you want to be mistaken for staff.

drink...

La Chope de *(top)*
Château Rouge
40 rue de Clignancourt, 18ème
Tel: 01 46 06 20 10
Open: daily, 6.30am–2am

Through no deliberate moves of its own, this down-at-heel bar, one of many on the rue de Clignancourt, has become *hyperbranché*, cited as a favourite by fashion editors and the like. Its mosaic floor tiles, plaster mouldings and nice-looking old classroom chairs have been adopted by cool kids, who flood in – and colonise the pavement outside – to socialise the night away. By day, with sunshine pouring in through the front windows, open to the street in summertime, it's an appealing place to linger for a few hours, with the 18ème arrondissement beeping and hollering away outside; don't forget your laptop. Drinks are cheap, and just €10 will buy you a plate of *andouillette grillée* and *tarte aux pommes*; they serve *couscous* every Thursday. On the whole, tons of fun.

Dédé la Frite *(middle)*
52 rue Notre-Dame-des-Victoires, 2ème
Tel: 01 40 41 99 90
Open: daily, 8am–2am

A dependably cool all-dayer, Dédé la Frite makes an unpretentious pitstop for the aperitif, with fairly priced wine and beers, and diner-style food served till 11pm: burgers, amazing hand-cut fries, grills and salads. It's easy to stay on 'til closing time, standing at the bar or occupying one of the dozen café tables, and bantering your way through a few bottles of wine. The decor is distressed and industrial, with exposed ducts, bare concrete and peeling paint. The crowd isn't quite as grungey, with lots of suits from the nearby Bourse coming by for after-work drinks, as well as indie boys in bashed-up leather jackets. The music's pretty ace too, starting out quirky and ending up loud.

De La Ville Café *(bottom)*
34 boulevard Bonne-Nouvelle, 10ème
Tel: 01 48 24 48 09
Open: daily, 11am–1.30am

The people behind Café Charbon (see page 104) rescued and refurbished this many-talented former brothel, handy as a pre-club or even instead-of-club venue near Grands Boulevards. It has something of a multiple personality, with a street-level terrace for daytime WiFiers, then a Belle Epoque bar inside, an industrial-baroque room with distressed walls, tables set out like a boho bistro, and further stairs to an art-gallery space. In a clubby nook at the rear, sauna-like pine cladding, padded seating in sex-district red and a clutch of taxidermy trophies create a surreal, where-are-we drinking den. The electro beats and a cast of nightlife creatures, more fascinating as the night unfolds, belie De La Ville's less atmospheric daytime incarnation. There's a restaurant menu, offering burgers, carpaccios and vegetarian antipasti, as well as a brunch *formule* at €20.

Les Editeurs *(top)*
4 carrefour de l'Odéon, 6ème
Tel: 01 43 26 67 76
Open: daily, 8am–2pm

For wholesome classicists, this library/restaurant/bar, located halfway between the Seine and the Jardin du Luxembourg, will seem natural and right, with its smart wooden panelling, spruce red leather chairs and highbrow references everywhere you glance. Hungover Romantics should find it even more of a tonic – there's nothing like a literary-leaning brunch to repair broken spirits. As well as wines by the glass, carafe and bottle, you can order *croque monsieur* or *madame* on *pain bio*, grilled baguette with *feta*, *tsatski* and *taramasalata*, or a full restorative monty of onion soup and steak tartare. Les Editeurs is, naturally, a great place to sit with a book or a newspaper, and is much frequented by the publishing-industry bigwigs for whom it is named.

Experimental *(middle)*
Cocktail Club
37 rue St-Sauveur, 2ème
Tel: 01 45 08 88 09
Open: daily, 7pm–2am (4am Thurs–Sat)

It may sound like a lab where your daiquiri comes in a test-tube, but this hip cocktail bar is done out in speakeasy style, with exposed brickwork, velvet drapes and leather bar stools. The drinks *are* experimental, albeit made with old-fashioned expertise: the Experience 1 combines vodka with lemon juice, basil, lemongrass and elderflower cordial; the Margarita uses agave nectar. Three young gents launched ECC in 2007, modelling their venture on their favourites in Manhattan, and hoping to improve Paris's go-dawful reputation among liquor lovers. There's nothing but a discreet sign to declare the bar to passers-by, apart from the bouncer… There's room for some 40 people inside; the clientele includes some impressively faithful regulars. The owners launched Curio Parlor in 2008, a bigger sibling venue in the Latin Quarter.

La Fourmi *(bottom)*
74 rue des Martyrs, 18ème
Tel: 01 42 64 70 35
Open: daily, 8am (10am Sun)–2am (4am Fri–Sat)

Scuffed ochre walls, industrial lamps, paintings by local artists – there's not much pretension about La Fourmi, where thirtysomething indie kids congregate for cheap beer and chat. It's a big old former bistro with high ceilings, generous windows and a long zinc bar that yields stacks of flyers, in case you're looking for a party; there are terrace tables, and some nice discreet nooks on the mezzanine level indoors. All resolutely untouristy, and authentically Parisian without being retro, unless you count the Bowie/Doors soundtrack. It fills up with party people at night, popular as a pre-club pub; by day, it does sterling work as a place to sit and read Derrida and nurse a coffee, or to collapse for an hour, during a hard day of Montmartre sightseeing.

drink…

Habibi *(top)*
44 rue Traversière, 12ème
Tel: 01 53 17 64 12
Open: 5pm–1am (2am Sat). Closed
Sundays.

Light years from Right Bank swank,
this tiny, freestyle corner wine bar near
Bastille, decked with cushions of many
colours, and low tables and chairs of
the recycled, make-do-and mend variety, thanks to the Senegalese artist who
had a hand in the design. Chez Habibi
has bags of scruffy charm, which suits
its crowd of regulars perfectly, and
it's often packed, even more so on
live-music nights and for the patron's
wine-tasting evenings. To accompany
the short but lipsmacking list of wines
by the glass, pichet and bottle, you can
order tapas, Provençal vegetable tart,
Corsican and Catalan charcuterie,
Thai and Indian *plats du jour* and puddings like fruity *clafoutis* or chocolate
moelleux.

Ice Kube *(middle)*
1–5 Passage Ruelle, Montmartre
Tel: 01 42 05 20 00
www.kubehotel.com
Open: daily, 7pm–2am. Ice bar open:
7pm–2am Wed–Sat; 7–11pm Sun.

Gimmicks are only daft if they are
unprofitable, and Kube hotel's ice bar
– where you mitten up for a half-hour
session on the Grey Goose vodka or
cocktails made therewith, for €38 admission (vodka included) – is super-
popular, so who'd knock it? Beneath
the chilly social hotspot there's a roomy
main bar, with DJs, squashy fake-fur
sofas and armchairs, dim lighting, and

a bar fringed with red LED lights. The
Kube complex (see Sleep) is hidden
behind gates on a titchy street near the
Gare du Nord. Grab a cab, rather than
stumbling in the dark, especially post-
vodka. And do book if you've got your
heart set on a sub-zero aperitif, since
space is limited.

Kong *(bottom)*
1 rue du Pont Neuf, 1er
Tel: 01 40 39 09 00 www.kong.fr
Open: daily, noon–2am (3am Fri–Sat)

A japanophile playground at the top of
the Kenzo flagship store near the Palais
Royal, this bar and restaurant offers a
quirky-glitzy alternative to hotel bars
and down-at-heel zincs. The Philippe
Starck look – all manga and light boxes
– is a bit tired, but a trip to Kong is still
a treat, in our view, especially at sunset,
or if you're carrying more than three
smart carrier bags and feeling a bit
Carrie Bradshaw. It's also a contender
for 'best Paris bar to forget about the
recession', thanks to the (unintention-
ally?) retro items on the Asian-fusion
snack menu, such as 'Glam Chic' to-
mato and mozzarella, and the 'Belle
& Zen' foie gras duo. A caipiroska or
a cosmopolitan will set you back a tidy
€15, but bear in mind you're paying for
one of the best views in Paris.

Lounge Bar *(left)*
Pershing Hall, 49 rue Pierre
Charron, 8ème
Tel: 01 58 36 58 00
www.pershinghall.com
Open: daily, 7pm–2am

If Costes is a pose too far, the bar at Pershing Hall boutique hotel (see Sleep) gets cocktail-hour glamour just right. The scale and grandeur of the rococo bar is perfect for the handsome room, and the pink and blue lighting creates a sensational, escapist impression. It's a pleasure to ascend the sweeping staircase, pass the restaurant (celebrated for its jungly vertical garden) and sip champagne among ruby-red Murano glass chandeliers and vases. If it all sounds rather classical, it ain't; the Andrée Putman design is boldly contemporary, and DJs set the place athrob most nights (there's a tiny dancefloor, in case the mood takes you). Clientele tend to be, or look like, media/fashion people, as fashion-conscious as you'd expect in this part of the world.

La Mezzanine *(top)*
de l'Alcazar
62 rue Mazarine, 6ème
Tel: 01 53 10 19 99 www.alcazar.fr
Open: daily, 7pm–2am

A sophisticated sibling to the Wagg club, just along the street, the Mezzanine de l'Alcazar is a hip cocktail bar, with a 1990s sort of vibe – but in a good way. All ages stand, sit, dance and flirt, dressy more or less, but not intimidatingly fashiony; a few suits fit in fine, as do jeans, though the girls are mainly kinda glam. Cocktails flow, and the music moves from afrofunk to Balearic to deep house and disco, intensifying as the evening develops; DJs play Wednesday to Saturday and, like Costes and Buddha Bar, La Mezzanine de L'Alcazar has released many volumes of branded CDs. On the walls is a selection of very cool art photography, curated by Michel Besmond, who set up L'Alcazar with Terence Conran 12 years ago (downstairs is a restaurant much like Quaglino's in London). The prints by Japanese eroticist Nobuyoshi Araki and underground Brooklynite Janine Gordon are all for sale.

La Palette *(right)*
43 rue de Seine, 6ème
Tel: 01 43 26 68 15
Open: daily, 8am–2am

Although a more grizzled clientele of gallery-owning types lunch on the *plat du jour* here, La Palette is predominantly a bar, and an essential one, at that. Jazz plays indoors, where proper aproned waiters come and go from the traditional zinc bar; the brown walls, old-school murals, caked painter's palettes and mirrors are all truly charming. But what you've really come for is the terrace, set just off the narrow rue de Seine, which always fills up by night with students from the nearby Ecole des Beaux-Arts, young American dilettantes and *bobo* types from all over Paris, smoking, talking and drinking Ricard and good wine. To leave any given subterranean den and come here for your last drink of the night is something like heaven.

La Patache
60 rue de Lancry, 10ème
Tel: 01 42 08 14 35
Open: daily, 6pm–2pm

Now that the famed Chez Prune has become a bit safe, we recommend this Second Empire drinking hole, which has, allegedly, been repainted since the 19th century but still looks as good as old. The yellow walls are adorned with sprigged wallpaper and right-on posters, and a wood-burning stove chuffs away in winter. The jukebox is no more than decorative, alas. If you want something simple and delicious to eat, you're in luck: La Patache's speciality is tinned food. No kidding: the *rillettes* are from the Vendée; the sardines from Morbihan; and it all comes with organic sourdough bread and *demi-sel* butter. What starts modestly here can end up all over the place, thanks to live music of all genres, improv theatre and the open, friendly vibe.

La Perle,
78 rue Vieille-du-Temple, 3ème
Tel: 01 42 72 69 93
Open: daily, 7am–2am (1am Sat/Sun)

A perky snapshot of young Paris, La Perle is an unmodernised 1970s café/ *tabac* that's been colonised by the cool kids but manages to retain a neighbourhood feel. It's at its most approachable in the mornings or on Sunday afternoon, but you'll have better fun if you include it on a Marais bar-crawl or stop by for a glass of (excellent) wine after an afternoon's shopping. La Perle's decor is astonishingly retro, with orange Formica walls, cube tables, Formica-veneered bar and booths at the back. The crowd is young, hot and talented/ambitious: actors, models, next big things, spillingly prettily onto the pavement in summer. Snacks are served, including, admirably, waffles with Nutella.

Le Petit Fer à Cheval
30 rue Vieille du Temple, 4ème
Tel: 01 42 72 47 47
www.cafeine.com
Open: daily, 8am–2am

Teeny-tiny, but big on atmosphere, Le Petit Fer à Cheval, named for its veritably horseshoe-shaped marble-topped bar, is 100 years old, and the recent retro fittings (giant mirrors, vintage posters) don't jar. Wait for your date at the front, watching the rue Vieille du Temple passing by or, if you're hungry, steal into the rear, where a dozen little tables await; breakfast comes with Mariage Frères tea, then there's steak tartare, fresh vegetable soup of the day, and a well-nigh miraculous vegetarian plate, as well as a charcuterie selection. Come at night, when it's less touristy. The cramped conditions, good mix of ages and unpredictable music policy make for gentle good fun.

Le Pin Up
13 rue Tiquetonne, 2ème
Tel: 01 42 33 04 86
Open: 5.30pm–2am (4am Fri–Sat).
Closed Sundays and Mondays.

A tiny-wee place in *flâneur*-friendly Montorgueil, very hipster, with white walls, retro furniture and boudoirish wallpaper. Like everywhere else on this street, it's welcoming to all comers, and the drinks don't cost silly money; cocktails are around €8. There's another whitewashed space downstairs, in the stone-vaulted basement, where DJs play Thursdays to Saturday, mainly electro but dependably good and diverse. Things hot up seriously at the weekend, with vintage-clad girls and bearded boys squeezing onto the size-small dancefloor. The staff try to keep the beats on the ground floor relatively gentle, so you can chat late into the night. The house cocktail is called the Piscine, and comes in a suitably big glass.

117

 **Au P'tit Garage** *(top)*
63 rue Jean-Pierre Timbaud,
11ème
Tel : 01 48 07 08 12
Open: daily, 6pm–2am

A sweetly shabby Oberkampf hangout that's pure rock 'n' roll – think Jesus & Mary Chain, not Bon Jovi – from the lurid 'Rock 'n' Roll High School' poster plastered on the scuffed red and yellow walls to the 1950s fridge (entirely decorative, we think) in the corner. Not to be confused with a real car workshop down a few doors on the same drag, Au P'tit Garage has three rooms: a former butchers, clothes store and, yes, a garage. The furniture is wonky and knackered, the music policy loud, alternative, anything but anodyne, and the clientele indie, friendly and full of post-gig gossip. If you like your beer with a chaser of Stiff Little Fingers or Siouxsie, or you're all luxed out and in need of a spot of grubby rehab, this ought to do the trick.

 Le Rendezvous *(middle)*
des Amis
23 rue Gabrielle, 18ème
Tel: 01 46 06 01 60
www.rdvdesamis.com
Open: daily, 8.30am–2am

Sacré Coeur may be the ultimate tourist-smothered honeypot, yet the streets only moments down to the west of the basilica make for a much cooler kind of day out – fashion and food retail, rather than Toulouse-Lautrec posters. It's nonetheless surprising to find this appealingly studenty corner café-bar directly beneath the city's bustliest attraction. It was, as the name suggest, set up by a group of pals, whose extended social circle eat, drink and chat here. The day-to-day clientele tends to be either very young or very old; those who drink here are touristic passersby or diehard regulars, of whom the bar is festooned with photographs. Cheese and charcuterie is available; the wine's good; and there's occasional live music in the back room. As we go to press the management is to change but, hopefully, this good-value, friendly little pitstop will remain warm and welcoming.

 Au Rocher *(bottom)*
de Cancale
78 rue Montorgueil, 2ème
Tel: 01 42 33 50 29
www.aurocherdecancale.fr
Open: daily, 8am–2am

Just north of Les Halles, the Montorgueil area has undergone stealthy gentrification in recent years, and is now a quarter of bourgeois charm, with lots of great food shops and fun places to eat and drink. Almost opposite legendary patisserie Stohrer is Au Rocher de Cancale, an unhectic neighbourhood hang-out where candles are lit, soul music plays and fine-looking locals chat on the terrace (replete with heaters for chilly evenings). The kitchen can rustle up 20 kinds of salad, such as Niçoise, Paysanne or the Cancale, with smoked salmon and mozzarella, and trad provincial dishes by night. It's all very laidback and, unless you stand on the street and survey the historic façade, it might come as a surprise that Parisians have been drinking here since 1846, especially when you clock the €4

vodka shots with Carambar on the cocktail list. The owners haven't been slavishly reverent towards the beamed interior, using it to exhibit young artists.

Le Rubis   (left)
10 rue du marché Saint-Honoré, 1er
Tel: 01 42 61 03 34
Open: 7am–10.30pm. Closed
Saturday evenings and Sundays.

Those who live for pure retro may gasp with pleasure when they set eyes on the red and cream 1950s interior – the real thing – of Le Rubis. The vintage light fittings, diner stools and wall-mounted wine list are all original, though the staff look far from likely to burst into a chorus of 'Beauty School Drop-out'. It's right on the cusp between the 1st and 2nd arrondissements, and serves a loyal clientele of regulars for *Poilâne* sandwiches and omelettes at lunchtime, and creative-industry locals later on. The appeal of this quirky, restrained little wine bar isn't based on nostalgia alone; it specialises in Loire and Beaujolais wines, with big-time Beaujolais Nouveau celebrations taking place in November, when the party spills out onto the street.

Le Verre Volé   (right)
67 rue Lancry, 11ème
Tel: 01 48 03 17 34
Open: noon–2.30pm; 7pm–11pm.
Closed Mondays. Shop open from
10am till late.

One for the purists, La Verre Volé is a temple to organic wines, aka a *cave à manger*, which sounds much nicer than 'off-licence you can eat in'. It's homely and to-the-point, and gives the distinct impression that profit isn't foremost in the owner's mind. The set-up is as follows: turn up, wait for a table if you forgot to reserve – there's only room for two dozen oenophiles– then drink *vins naturels* by the glass or get stuck into any bottle from the outstanding retail selection lining the walls (€6 corkage). You have to eat, for licencing reasons, but that's no hardship. Excellent sausages, charcuterie, cheese, oysters, etc, are brought in from the best local traiteurs. The retail side is healthy, to say the least; the door flies open every few minutes, as someone nips in to grab a bottle of Gigondas to take home for supper. N.B.: if you come early, you're more likely to get a walk-in.

Zéro Zéro   (bottom)
89 rue Amelot, 11ème
Tel: 01 49 23 51 00
Open: daily, 6pm–2am

If you could wear this Bastille bar, it would be a Ramones T-shirt. Zéro Zéro is ten years old but still kicking. Boys in leather jackets and girls with fringes flirt darkly, mainly outdoors, since it's so darn small: a miniscule street-level drinking hole drawing an electro/indie crowd that ends up four-thick on Thursdays and Fridays. There's not much to see (the decor hasn't been refurbished in living memory), except for a blackboard bearing good news: an extensive cocktail list, including the Zéro Zéro, a whoop-ass pick-me-up of rum, ginger and lime. Happy hour is now advertised between 6.30pm and 8pm, but the way of the world is that you probably won't find yourself here much before midnight.

snack...

Parisians do like to stick to their regimented meal times and, no less, to spend long hours languishing over three- and four-course extravaganzas, so snacking isn't a fully realised concept here. You only have to witness the admirable French capacity for remaining model-slim to grasp that this is not a nation of grazers.

The obvious candidates for all-day eating are the classic brasseries and café-bars, where there's almost always a steak, a goat's cheese salad or a *croque monsieur* to be had. For the ultimate hedonist's snack – a dozen oysters and a bottle of something cold and white – seek out the more glamorous brasseries with shell-fish counters, such as Lutétia on boulevard Raspail or La Coupole on boulevard Montparnasse.

If you feel moved to stray from the familiar clichés, it can be tricky to find a light lunch after 2pm, unless you find yourself in either a department store (Le Bon Marché, Printemps, Galeries Lafayette) or one of the non-French areas. The old Jewish quarter of the Marais, around rue des Rosiers, is recommended for unbeatable *falafel*, as well as kosher pizza round the clock, and poppy-seed cake from Korcarz bakery. You'll find syrup-soaked Middle Eastern pastries in the tearoom at the Mosquée de Paris and, in overwhelming variety, at La Bague de Kenza, where rue Saint-Maur meets Oberkampf.

One excellent new development is the deli-with-tables. Instead of window-licking of a lunchtime, you can now sit down at *epicerie-restos* such as Bread & Roses, Granterroirs, Aux Pipalottes Gourmandes and celebrated Anglo-French success story Rose Bakery, to eat fresh salads, home-made pies and tarts.

Pink Flamingo

Alternatively, if you can push on through till teatime, you'll discover that Paris is a city obsessed with rare teas (specialists include La Maison des Trois Thés in the 5ème, Le Palais des Thés on rue Vieille du Temple and Les Contes de Thé in Saint-Germain-des-Prés). Cake is no less serious a preoccupation. The reverence with which master *pâtissiers* are spoken of is matched only by the extravagance of their creations, with the grand hotels competing furiously to outdo one another's teatime spread.

Again, a cake shop where you can indulge on the spot is a rarity, which suggests either that eclairs are a luxury to be offered to friends, or that Parisians prefer not to scoff custard in public. For sit-down treats, each of the four Mariage Frères shops houses a *salon de thé*, where you can have your cake and eat it, or there's the ultimate, Ladurée, credited as pastry consultant on Sofia Coppola's 2006 film *Marie Antoinette.*

Alas, no seating, but the ancient and gilded bakery called Du Pain et des Idées, on the corner of rue Yves Toudic and rue de Marseille in the 10ème, is a fairytale place to pick up sweet *brioche* to eat by the Canal Saint-Martin. Boulangerie Arnaud Delmontel on rue des Martyrs is a former winner of the Croissant of the Year award, and an errand to make time for when you're leaving town via the Gare du Nord. Picnicking is a summer-time pastime in itself, with locals favouring the banks of the Seine, the canalside and the pedestrian Pont des Arts over the parks. With staggeringly good delis on every street, it's not hard to create a fabulous alfresco feast but, if it's beyond you to buy a baguette and a chuck of Comté, head to the Canal Saint-Martin's Pink Flamingo, which will convey piping-hot organic pizza to your chosen canalside spot by bicycle.

Angelina's *(left)*

226 rue du Rivoli, 1er
Tel: 01 42 60 82 00
Open: daily, 9am–7pm

Located as it is, between Place Vendôme and the Louvre, its entrance under the colonnade opposite the Jardin des Tuileries, Café Angelina was never going to be any kind of secret. Honestly, the queues are such, you might dismiss it as a tourist trap. But don't strop off to look for somewhere emptier – enjoy the appetising wait. Beyond the shop selling biscuits, jams and pâtisserie, sweet-toothed pilgrims sit in the grand tearoom, among gilded mouldings, great murals and mirrors. Everything is charmingly worn, from the red carpet to the brown leather chairs and green marble tables, constantly occupied by dozens of happy cake eaters. The waiters try to play up to the off-hand Parisian stereotype, but can't help actually being helpful and considerate. Then, of course, there's the reason you're there: sugary pastries and sublime hot chocolate. Both are yumsters, and worth the steep prices, but do go strictly either-or, unless you've literally just walked around the whole Louvre.

Big Ben Bar *(top)*

Gare de Lyon, 12ème
Tel: 01 43 43 09 06
www.le-train-bleu.com
Open: daily, 7:30am (9am Sun)–11pm

An extravagantly beautiful backdrop, albeit one with an incongruous cast of average folk waiting for the 10.44 to Grenoble, this café/bar occupies the end of the historic Train Bleu restaurant (see EAT). A long, carpeted, suitably train-like corridor leads from the main restaurant, with a room off to the side for waiting, people-watching and tucking into smoked salmon with dill Chantilly and blinis (€28), Caesar salad (€23) or the 'formule teatime' (€16). They do a decent full English breakfast, as well as the Continental kind; brunch is offered on Sunday, though not during midsummer. You can eat till around 8pm; top-drawer teas and good if costly cocktails take you up to closing time. The faded grandeur of this elegant time-warp is a must if you're travelling to or from the Gare de Lyon. The indistinct train noises and announcements make it very *Brief Encounter*, and the ladies' loo is just something else.

Bread & Roses *(right)*

7 rue de Fleurus, 6ème
01 42 22 06 06
Open: 8am–8pm. Closed Sundays.

Who'd have thought that among the biggest raves on the current Paris food scene is a deli both both humble and English-influenced? Bread & Roses is a huge hit among locals for its fresh, organic bread (the fruit and rye varieties are particularly lauded), healthy yet delicious salads, huge puff-pastry tarts and sublime cheesecake. The light-filled corner site has a stone floor and cherry-wood furniture, and there's room for 18 people, plus seats at a handful of tables on the street. Prices are high, but the well-heeled residents of the 6ème don't seem to mind; they're enthused by lighter, simpler lunching, and this is *the* place to get birthday cakes. Come for breakfast or Saturday brunch, and look out for celeb devotees, such as Catherine Deneuve and Emmanuelle Béart.

Le Café *(left)*
62 rue Tiquetonne, 2ème
01 40 39 08 00
Open: daily, 10am–2am Mon–Sat; noon–midnight Sun

An unpretentious treasure whose prosperity has risen with its adoption by a trendy crowd, Le Café is an impeccably hip, old-school spot to stop for a breather in the gentrified Montorgueil district. The few pavement tables are particularly prized. The owner is a well-travelled gent, and the colonial-style interior is decorated with bits and bobs from around the world, as well as globes, maps and tatty travel posters. Light salads, *tartines* and *croques monsieurs* (really good ones, made with a choice of breads) are on offer by day; at the weekend, come nightfall, house and electro music begins to throb, and the scene spills out onto the street.

Café le Basile *(top)*
34 rue Grenelle, 7ème
Tel: 01 42 22 59 46
Open: 7am–9.30pm (8pm Sat). Closed Sundays.

On one hand, this nonchalant retro café is a New Wave film come to life, thanks to its young clientele of Sciences Po students and profs from the *faculté* over the road; on the other, it's a godsend for weary shoppers, bang in the middle of rue Grenelle, where half a dozen luxury-brand shoe designers congregate. An unpretentious, youthful spot for a beer and a croque monsieur, it comes with a Daft Punk/ hip-hop soundtrack, sports on a small screen, and oversized 1960s rock portraits hanging over the Formica tables, red banquettes and 1950s prints. At the front, you can stand at a glossy red and yellow bar, or perch on red-topped stools at high tables; there's plenty of room at the back for intellectualising and flirting.

Café Beaubourg *(right)*
100 rue Saint-Martin, 4ème
Tel: 01 48 87 63 96
Open: daily, 7am–1am Sun–Thurs; 9am–2am Fri–Sat

With a wide-angle view of the Pompidou Centre's plaza and its happenings, this café has become a classic since it was opened by the Costes brothers in 1985; once hip, it is now more of a BCBG pitstop. Its modern design is holding up well, especially now it's beginning to look a bit retro. On a sunny day, the terrace tables and chairs in white steel and coloured plastic are colonised completely by members of the chattering classes and users of the free WiFi. Inside, white-marble floors, concrete columns and modern art make for a cerebral yet chilled-out brasserie, where solitary intellos have lunch with their laptops, and black-clad waiters stride to and fro bearing cocktails, salads, and steak *tartare poelé*. There's tons of space, with a sweeping, polished concrete staircase leading to a second floor.

Café Fleurus *(left)*
2 rue de Fleurus, 6ème
Tel: 01 45 44 79 79
Open: 7am (8am Sat)–7.30pm. Closed
Sundays.

A skip from the Jardin de Luxembourg, this unpretentious *tabac-café* is light and airy, with retro fittings such as pink Perspex shapes overhead and mono-chrome harlequin screen-prints on the walls. A young crowd sits on ban-quettes at white Formica tables, served by men who seem to have worked here for generations. It's a perfect place to start the day, rest up after a tour of the APC fashion emporium opposite (see Shop), or head to for a snack and a beer after a walk in the park. A simple menu of cheese plates, omelettes and sandwiches is on offer, and for break-fast there's the *pâtisserie du jour*. Six sunny sidewalk tables are hotly con-tested, year-round.

Café de l'Industrie *(bottom)*
16–17 rue St-Sabin, 11ème
Tel: 01 47 00 13 53
Open: daily, 9am–2.30am

Not as white-hot as it was five years ago, when it was wall-to-wall with the Bastille's young writers and designers, this trendy neighbourhood bistro, with its utility-chic details and walls hung with old movie-star portraits, is none-theless still a trusty all-dayer, and veri-tably buzzes at lunch and dinner. The menu is French and unfussy and offers a good choice at decent prices; the puddings, especially the chocolate *mi-cuit*, are worth making yourself late for. So successful is the Café de l'Industrie

formula, the proprietors have ex-panded not just into the premises of a former Moroccan restaurant over the road, but also, surprisingly, into a linge-rie boutique next door, where you get five per cent off if you precede your knicker-shopping with an onion soup and a tuna steak.

Cafés et Thés Verlet *(right)*
266 rue Saint-Honoré, 1er
Tel: 01 42 60 67 39
www.cafesverlet.com
Open: 9.30am–6.30pm. Closed
Sundays.

A quiet, unhurried experience, Verlet is a connoisseur's coffee house, set back one street from the teeming rue du Rivoli. Stocking dozens of single-plan-tation coffees and premium teas, it's a veritable temple to caffeine. There's room for 20 in the rustic-style salon downstairs, which is bedecked with all manner of tea and coffee ephem-era; upstairs feels more contemporary, with a huge window looking out over rue Saint-Honoré. If you'd care to be guided among the brews on offer, owner (and roaster extraordinaire) M Duchossoy, who bought the business from Pierre Verlet, grandson of the founder, is happy to guide customers through his handpicked selection. He knows many of his producers by name, including the Cameroonian Catholic monks who make his washed Arabica Peaberry. If you like what you try, you can buy a bag to take home with you; there's a mail order service, too.

Chez *Jeannette*

L'ÉTABLISSEMENT
N'ACCEPTE PAS
LES CHÈQUES.

LA MAISON NE
FAIT PAS CRÉDIT
MERCI DE VOTRE
COMPRÉHENSION

La Charlotte de l'Isle *(left)*
24 rue Saint-Louis-en-l'Ile, 4ème
Tel: 01 43 54 25 83 www.la-charlotte.fr
Open: 2–8pm Thurs–Sun

A place of pilgrimage on the Ile St Louis, a fairytale come to life, presided over by eccentric chocolatière and poetess, Madame Sylvie Langlet. Her teashop is full to the brim with bemusing artefacts, carnival masks, witches on broomsticks, gnomes and marionettes (which come alive during her puppet shows every Wednesday, by reservation only). She has been serving her potent hot chocolate for more than 30 years at tables in the front room and tiny parlour; it is almost narcotic, and comes in a pretty jug, served with a glass of water. Home-made treats include a lightly spiced carrot cake with chocolate crust. If you ask to use the loo in the rear courtyard, you get to glimpse Madame's magical chocolatey kitchen, where she makes her edible sculptures.

Chez Jeannette *(bottom)*
47 rue du Faubourg-Saint-Denis, 10ème
Tel: 01 47 70 30 89
Open: daily, 8am–2am

A shabby-chic (it really is both) zinc bar, bought from the eponymous Jeannette two years ago by a hip young cabal, this neon-lit hang-out serves trad French fare by day, chalked up on the blackboard – *assiette de charcuterie*, *bavette poelée* – and switches into party mode by night and at the weekend. Opposite Passage Brady, where Indian restaurants compete for trade, its decaying interior is reminiscent of cafés found today only in Havana or Mumbai. The clientele's average age has plummeted since the trendy takeover, but nothing much else has changed, from the yellowing wallpaper to the Chez Jeannette sign over the bar. Come for a plate of cheese and a *pichet de blanc* around 6pm or 7pm, while it's still easy-going and you can squeeze into a booth at the back; return later to see it kick off, socially speaking.

La Contrescarpe *(right)*
57 rue Lacépède, 5ème
Tel: 01 43 36 82 88
Open: daily, 7am–2am

Apart from its fine big terrace overlooking the famous square of Place de la Contrescarpe, once home to Ernest Hemingway and now host to occasional jazz concerts in summer, this café doesn't look particularly exceptional from the outside. Indoors, though, it's a classic, with three seating areas to choose from: an 'English-style' library at the front, with dark walnut bookshelves, green walls and squishy brown-leather club chairs; a light-filled dining room with wicker chairs, off which is hidden a discreet drinking den, with low, cushioned seating; and, finally, a delightful little patio with generously spaced tables and bushy shrubs. The kitchen turns out bistro favourites such as great chicken and chips and confit de canard; locals and tourists devour bargain lunch menus (from €16), while students spend hours chatting away on leather banquettes.

snack…

La Galerie des Gobelins
(bottom)

Hôtel Plaza Athénée, 25 avenue Montaigne, 8ème
Tel: 01 53 67 66 65
www.plaza-athenee-paris.com
Open: daily, 8am–1am

To us, they're just (very nice) cakes, but to become pastry chef at the Plaza Athénée is equivalent in France to the highest sporting or scientific achievements. Pierre Michalak has trained with the best (Ladurée, Pierre Hermé), won championships, impressed Jacques Chirac and experimented with profiteroles. His playful creations have recently included cherry and orange-flower 'frisbee' macaroons; *religieuses* on chocolate skateboards; and chocolate and salted-caramel sailing boats. To take tea here, you walk from the impressive lobby, past the gastronomic restaurant, to a wide corridor, aka the Galerie des Gobelins, overlooking the hotel's central courtyard. Here, business meetings and wide-eyes tourists alike are plied with delicacies beneath crystal chandeliers. Apart from all the sugar-spun genius, the menu features salade niçoise, black spaghetti with lobster, the *croque-plaza* (chicken and truffle) and super-duper cocktails. Dress up a smidge.

Granterroirs
(right)

30 rue de Miromesnil, 8ème
Tel: 01 47 42 18 18
www.granterroirs.com
Open: noon–3pm Mon–Fri (shop open 9am–8pm)

With room for 60 at its communal oak tables, the dining room of this Aladdin's Cave of regional gastro goodies is an admirable enterprise, offering robust daily specials, such as penne with truffle and cèpes, cassoulet and osso buco, and unbelievably good puddings (the horn of plenty with berries and exotic fruits is the stuff of legend). Granterroirs has been going for 10 years as an *épicerie fine*, specialising in the very best produce from all over France, hence the name. Foie gras from Périgord, tapenade from Provence, wine from small domaines, dozens of mustards and jams… As well as sitting down to lunch (private dinners by arrangement), you can get your kicks browsing among the 800 delicacies in stock; buying presents for the food-lovers in your life doesn't get much more enjoyable.

Ladurée
(left)

75 avenue des Champs-Elysées, 8ème
Tel : 01 40 75 08 75 www.laduree.fr
Open: daily, 8.30am (8am Sun) –midnight

A legend in its own teatime, the Champs Elysées Ladurée is, for our money, the one to come to, since you can combine it with a gawp at the gilded interior of the Guerlain flagship spa over the road. A fabulous Second Empire stage set, it is the biggest and most splendid of three Ladurée teahouses in Paris. The original opened in 1862 on 16 rue Royale (the other two are cunning fabrications), and there's a third in St-Germain-des-Prés. The one thing they all have in common is the long counter, lit by neoclassical statuettes holding lampshades, where the famous

macaroons, those nibbled by fashion editors and celebs, are laid out daily to tempt all comers. Upstairs is a baby-blue room fit for a princess (plus entourage), complete with grandfather clock, candelabra and gilded mirrors. A dimly lit, chinoiserie-themed central room, a small 'library' and two more dining rooms are connected by way of a long, creaky, wooden-floored corridor, leading finally to plush bathrooms. What to eat? Cake, cake and cake. Take some macaroons home with you.

Lô Sushi *(left)*
8 rue de Berri, 8ème
Tel: 01 45 62 01 00 www.losushi.com
Open: noon–4pm, 7pm–12.30am
Mon–Fri; noon–12:30am Sat/Sun

Useful and fun, this cheerful, polished *kaiten* sushi joint is a miracle if you're struck by hunger on the Champs-Élysées. During the week, well-heeled local workers pluck quality sushi and sashimi from the conveyor belt; at the weekends, Parisian parents bring their young; the Andrée Putman decor incorporates unintrusive video footage on wall-mounted screens, and music plays at an atmosphere-enhancing volume. The sushi verges on luxurious, with teriyaki foie gras and scallop carpaccio, as well as tuna maki, California rolls and seaweed salad, all priced according to the colour of the plates, from €3 to €11.

Le Loir dans *(bottom)*
la Théière
3 rue des Rosiers, 4ème
Tel: 01 42 72 90 61

Open: 9.30am–7pm Mon–Fri

On one of the Marais' most trottable shopping streets, great for *falafels* and fashion, this coffee shop is always crammed absolutely to the gunwales; don't bet on getting a table, and hang onto it for a few hours when you do. The name is an Alice in Wonderland reference (dormouse/teapot) and the two large, homely rooms are festooned with suitable murals, as well as vintage show posters and random character-adding bric-à-brac. There are 18 varieties of tea on offer, and excellent home-made cakes – mighty chocolate cake, a trembling slab of lemon meringue pie – are delivered to the scruffy tables by unflappable staff. The tarts and sandwiches are great too; this place would be perfect, if only it weren't so busy…

snack…

Mamie Gateaux *(right)*
66 rue du Cherche-Midi, 6ème
Tel: 01 42 22 32 15
www.mamie-gateaux.com
Open: 11.30am–6pm. Closed Sundays and Mondays.

Perfectly adorable, from the tiny madeleine that comes with your tea (try the bourbon vanilla) to the wooden school furniture, this dear little establishment is part of a mini Mamie Gateaux empire, starting with the tearoom, and continuing next door to a boutique, rather reminiscent of east London's Labour & Wait, and a *brocante* selling nostalgic school-related collectibles. The owners, a French/Japanese couple, have recreated a vanishing *grandmère* style of Frenchness to very comforting effect. The tarts, soups, salads and cakes are all home-made, and the menu is printed on a leaf of paper designed to look as though it's pulled from an exercise book. You can buy teas and jams to take home, and the prices in the *brocante* are nice and old-school, too.

Mariage Frères *(left)*
30 rue du Bourg Tibourg, 4ème
Tel: 01 42 72 28 11
www.mariagefreres.com
Open: daily, noon–7pm (shop opens 10.30am)

This establishment is as essential as Brasserie Lipp or the Eiffel Tower, and all the more precious since there isn't an outlet in London or the US (lots in Japan, though). France's first importers of tea (est. 1660) opened their original teahouse and shop on the narrow Marais rue du Bourg Tibourg in 1854, and have been supplying chic Parisians with their special brews ever since. Serious tea-drinkers wouldn't dream of coming to Paris without spending an hour here, not only to sit in the colonial-style tearoom, but also to stock up on their favourite Darjeelings and Earl Greys to take home. Hundreds of black tea cans line the oak shelves, and you can lean over the counter and stick your snout into each and every one of them, time and patience permitting; in the old-fashioned style, you pay at a kiosk, once your purchase has been packaged. The salon offers the same cosmic selection of tea, as well as tea-scented cakes, light snacks and salads. Three other tea rooms have opened in the 6ème and 8ème, at 13 rue des Grands Augustins; 260 faubourg Saint-Honoré; and 17 place de la Madeleine.

Café Maure de la *(right)* Mosquée de Paris
29 rue Geoffroy Saint-Hilaire, 5ème
Tel: 01 43 31 38 20
www.la-mosquee.com
Open: daily, 10am–11.30pm (kitchen closes 10.30pm)

This peaceful mosque, founded in 1920, and adjacent to the Institut du Monde Arabe, is open to both Muslims and non-Muslims, who come largely to enjoy the bookshop, *hammam* and tearoom. During the summer, you can sip your *thé à la menthe* in a lovely tree-shaded courtyard and read or chat to the sound of birdsong; in winter, it's all about lounging on cushioned benches among horseshoe arches, pot-bellied lamps and copper tray tables. Friendly waiters pour the sugary fresh-mint tea from a great height into traditional tea glasses, and keep the calorific, sticky pastries coming, It's an escapist experience, owing to the mosque's Moorish architecture; Moroccan, Algerian and Tunisian craftsmen were employed in creating the interior, with its polychrome faience tiles, porphyry stone fountains and cedarwood doors.

Pink Flamingo *(bottom)*
67 rue Bichat, 10ème
01 42 02 31 70
www.pinkflamingo.com
Open: noon–3pm, 7–11pm Tues–Fri; 1–11pm Sat/Sun. Closed Mondays.

This inspired pizza joint's hands-on owners are full of brilliant ideas. First, the pizza's thin bases are made with organic flour and virgin olive oil; and the imaginative toppings range

snack...

from eight cheeses (the Cantona) to chicken, prawns and saffron (the Almodóvar). Second, you can order your pizza, then go and sit by the canal (Pink Flamingo's just round the corner from Quai Valmy) and await for your bicycle delivery, holding the helium balloon they give you so they can spot you. If your 'pink-nik' is kyboshed by by the weather, there's a dinky dining room next door to the takeaway counter and kitchen. The look is fluoro rock 'n' roll: you can't miss the black and pink exterior with its pink-flamingo sign. There's a second outlet in the Marais, at 105 rue Vieille du Temple, and they opened in Berlin in 2009. Also new in 2009 was the Obama pizza, with grilled bacon and pineapple chutney.

Aux Pipalottes Gourmandes *(left)*
49 rue Rochechouart, 9ème
Tel: 01 44 53 04 53
Open: daily, noon–9.30pm (deli open 10am–11pm)

A clever deli that has made room for eating, as well as gastronomic consumerism, Aux Pipalottes Gourmandes is high on the list of excellent traiteurs and bakeries that make this corner of the 9ème arrondissement such a foodie destination. You can sample the goods at one of seven tables in the middle of the room, surrounded by shelves of attractively packaged foodstuffs, or perched outside on the pavement. The deli counter at the front is heaving with freshly made delectables, from ever-popular nems to classic vegetable terrine. It's such a hit with locals, who tend to accompany their snacking with carefully selected bottle of wine,

that you can even book. Be warned: it's almost impossible to resist buying the entire contents of the shop on your way out.

Place Verte *(right)*
105 rue Oberkampf, 11ème
Tel: 01 43 57 34 10
Open: daily, 10am–2am

The youthful party scene around rue Oberkampf doesn't wake up till the evening but, even by day, there's life at Place Verte, a multifunctional, creative space with a friendly, laidback vibe. It's an expansive interior, with a bar to the front, dispensing cocktails, smoothies and hot chocolate, tables where young families and solitary laptop-tappers can hang out for the afternoon, a greenery-filled vitrine at the rear, and a salad bar in the middle. You can order pizza, pasta, soup of the day, or fancier dishes such as rare tuna with Espelette pepper; by night, it's more of a bar scene, with live music and DJs at weekends. Provided you're into vaguely lefty 1970s hang-outs, you can't go wrong here. There's a 'long, hot summer' clause, too: a big, shady terrace crammed with colourful plastic chairs.

Pozzetto *(bottom)*
39 rue du Roi de Sicile, 4ème
Tel: 01 42 77 08 64 www.pozzetto.biz
Open: daily, noon–11pm

In-the-know Parisians will tell you that neither Amorino nor their own Berthillon is king of the cones, but that Pozzetto serves up the best ice cream in Paris, possibly the world. Here, in his Italian caffè gelato in the Marais, the

LE PETIT DEJEUNER FAMILIAL

BANANIA

snack...

bafflingly slender patron will offer you the choice of a dozen freshly made flavours (*melone, fior di latte, marrons glacés*). The spruce shop is the picture of a contemporary candy store, with graphic-print flooring underfoot and a hot-pink back wall. If ice cream isn't your thing, the coffee and hot chocolate are both amazing, and the small selection of goods for sale includes stupendous chocolate and hazelnut spread.

....

Rose Bakery (below)
46 rue des Martyrs, 9ème
Tel: 01 42 82 12 80
Open: 10am–6pm. Closed Mondays.

A fashion-world favourite for yonks (there's a concession in London's hip Dover Street Market), Rose Bakery has recesssion-chic appeal, thanks to its fresh, good-quality fare and minimal style. A fixture on the foodie trail that runs up and down rue des Martyrs/rue Rochechouart, it's a humble converted *chartil* (a market trader's fruit and veg lock-up, basically) with concrete floors, whitewashed walls and room for about 30 people. Rose and Jean-Charles (she's English; he's French) bring a farmer's market sensibility to lunchtime, and bake anglophile treats for teatime. Their salads, tarts, Eccles cakes and carrot cake *always* run out. Locals love it, and Brits and Americans are delighted by the shelves of British groceries, and a smashing brunch of bacon and eggs, boiled eggs with Marmite toast, kedgeree or porridge.

Café de l'Industrie

party...

The nightlife scene in Paris is in rude health. Fun is high on the agenda; French dance music continues to compensate for the Johnny Hallyday years; and the rest of northern Europe has stopped tutting at the Parisian habit of chucking in a bit of Cure or loungecore during a house set, and joined in. Just be aware that a bar atmosphere often prevails, unless we're talking hard-dancing techno, and that many club nights kick off with a live band, so don't leave before the DJ starts, thinking you're in the wrong joint. Another thing to keep in mind is that many of the coolest nights are all but impossible to get into, unless you know the right people – but of course you do, don't you?

It's a tale of two cities, largely: a clubbing scene polarised by money. On one hand, you've got the unashamedly glitzy venues, more or less old-school, such as Mathis, Chez Tania and Le Bar. These are for Formula One drivers and A-list entertainers, as well as scions of the ruling families of France and elsewhere. Then, there are the progressive, creative spaces, such as Point Ephémère and La Bellevilloise, where clubbing meets art, performance, video, etc, under the umbrella of adventurous programming; these sometimes win public funding, but don't let that put you off – the French are officially culturally sophisticated, remember...

There is another strand of nightlife between the flashy and the left-field, the supertrendy scene around Le Baron and Le Régine and the now defunct Paris Paris, led by the cabal of party-loving creatives who are also associated with Hotel Amour (see Sleep). Wherever they lead, international fashion/design youth follow. If you're simply looking for a dance, once the bars close at 2am, there are easier places to get into. Clubs such as Wagg and Queen are your best bet for cheesy good times and Kylie medleys; Le Rex and Folie's Pigalle are among the most respected temples to house music and attract big-name DJs. Indie nightlife is alive and well, especially around rue Oberkampf, though pop kids tend to congregate in bars and live-music venues; electro music has taken over as the default soundtrack for twentysomething Paris.

Gay Paris is thriving all-round, thanks in part to the city's openly gay mayor Bertrand Delanoé. There are gay clubs nights here and there, but the dozens of bars and cafés in the Marais are really where it's at; Open Café is a good place to start. The lesbian scene is centred around the crossroads of rue du Roi de Sicile and rue des Etouffes in the south Marais. In general, most clubs open at midnight and close around 6am at weekends; if admission isn't free, you'll usually pay between €12 and €20, and sometimes there's a free drink thrown in.

party...

Showcase

Le Baron *(left)*
6 avenue Marceau, 8ème
Tel: 01 47 20 04 01
www.clublebaron.com
Open: daily, around 11pm–late

With one of the severest door policies in Paris (you'd better be Facebook friends with at least one regular), Le Baron has ruled the roost since it opened in 2004. Its acts seedy decor – it was a brothel in a former life – resounds to 1980s pop and live bands every night of the week, with Mondays just as riotous as weekends. Vintage posters, featuring cavorting semi-clad nymphs, are lit by the rosy glow of tasselled lamps, hanging above red couches and a dozen candlelit round tables, which are more or less reserved for regulars; the venue holds 150 revellers max, so you'll be probably find yourself edged onto the diminutive, jampacked dancefloor. Run by the same team as Chez Regine, Le Baron is more of a jumping bar than a club but, whatever you call it, it's one of the city's highest-status nightspots. Since it can be a palaver to get in, make sure you look hot, and keep a Plan B up your Lanvin sleeve.

La Bellevilloise *(bottom)*
19 rue Boyer, 20ème
Tel: 01 46 36 07 07
www.labellevilloise.com
Open: 5.30pm–2am Wed–Fri;
11am–2am Sat–Sun

Four storeys and 2,000sq/m of cross-cultural creativity, Le Bellevilloise is an arty, *multitendance* community centre of cool, which puts on hundreds of events a year, from debates and film festivals to Afrobeat and electro club nights. The building (and the name) previously belonged to a worker's co-op, and the people power continues. Its artistic programming is definitely taken seriously – a number of their do's have been supported by the Ministry of Culture – but imagination and wit are always in the house. As well as a restaurant, terrace, club/concert venue and cutting-edge audiovisual, gallery and event spaces, there are always new ideas, such as a recently installed indoor lawn with hammocks, deckchairs, a pop-up library and masseurs. It's like a bit of Berlin in the 20th, where all comers are invited to overstep cultural boundaries. It's fun and friendly, too, and the musical offerings tend to be top-quality.

Black Calvados *(right)*
40 avenue Pierre
1er de Serbie, 8ème
Tel: 01 47 20 77 77 www.bc-paris.fr
Open: 10pm–2am. Closed Sundays.

A black lacquered box upstairs (the bar), a polished metal box downstairs (the club), this deceptive old-timer, a swinging-era haunt of Serge Gainsbourg's, has been pinged into the 21st century with new ownership. Hot as long ago as the 1950s, and subsequently a favourite among the permatanned classes, it's now attracting a younger crowd of Parisian and international twentysomethings (still well-heeled, since we're minutes away from the Georges V and the Champs Elysées). Entry is free and it's 'open to all', though in reality the door's not as penetrable as all that. Champagne or a cocktail costs around €15. The music policy combines hard rock and electro

party...

to storming effect, and the best nights are Tuesday and the weekend.

....

Castel *(left)*
15 rue Princesse, 6ème
Tel: 01 40 51 52 80
www.castel-paris.abcsalles.com
Open: 9pm–dawn Tues–Sat

Amanda Lear first met Salvador Dalí at Castel, which rivalled Régine as the swingingest hang-out in 1960s Paris. New owners took over at the end of the Nineties, and paid their respects to its late founder by changing very little: the warren of red-velvet salons and two restaurants continue to provide an intimate St-Germain watering hole for film and fashion people and, unless you're Jack Nicholson or Jack White, you'd better know a regular if you want to join in. The music policy is angled towards disco and funk – nothing too moody – and there's an unofficial dress code of relaxed chic for her and a decent suit for him. Dinner is served from 9pm, and the nightclub kicks off at midnight.

....

Le ChaCha *(bottom)*
47, rue Berger, 1er
Tel: 01 40 13 12 12
www.chachaclub.fr
Open: 8pm–5am. Closed Sundays.

Le ChaCha opened in 2008, a new venture from the people behind the likable and laidback Hotel du Nord restaurant on the Canal St Martin (see Eat). It's a civilised affair in terms of its restaurant, where you can book to eat carpaccio and *carré d'agneau*; the bar, *fumoir* and music room play host to more unpredictable pleasures, from burlesque nights to after-parties for Givenchy, Royksopp and so on. The interior is the antithesis of scruffy-dive style, a series of subtly lit rooms with mirrors, rich textiles and an air of 1930s elegance. During the Cannes Film Festival in spring 2009, the club decamped to the Riviera and hosted the party of the season, aka Le Cha-Cha Beach.

....

Chez Carmen *(right)*
53 rue Vivienne, 2ème
Tel: 01 42 36 45 41
Open: midnight–9am (noon Sat).
Closed Sundays.

The look of this bar-cum-club is nothing memorable; it's simply a square, mirrored room with a bar to one side. But at four in the morning (don't come here before then) it'll be so packed and you'll be so drunk that you simply won't care. Loud house music is played to a crowd still reeling happily from whichever venue they've just been chucked out of. They don't want to go home, they want to party hard – and they can do it here, until the last person either leaves or falls over. Chez Carmen is perfect for insomniacs or those with an early-morning Eurostar to catch. You won't remember getting here or leaving, but you'll have a feeling you've just done something fun.

party...

Le Divan du Monde   *(left)*
75 rue des Martyres, 18ème
Tel: 01 40 05 06 99
www.divandumonde.com
Open: 11.30pm–6am Fri/Sat (check
website for weekday openings)

Club, bar, concert venue and art space,
Le Divan du Monde is all about cultural cross-pollination, putting on regular nights where video, dance, short
films and DJ sets meet experimentally
and enthusiastically. The interior is a
strange mix of cosy and creative, with
its arty fittings and old-school/organic
design. From 11pm onwards, the main
space is usually closed, and the upstairs bar, technically called Le Divan
Japonais, fills up with Montmartre folk
who've come to kick back with friends
to the sound of glitchy electronica.
Once or twice a week, the two floors
come alive simultaneously, to create a
club for 500 people; the baroque decor
of the theatre and the more modern
balcony area work well together. The
music policy adventures beyond the
electro *du jour*, with gypsy, rai and punk
all getting a look in.

Le Duplex   *(right)*
25 rue Michel-le-Comte, 3ème
Tel: 01 42 72 80 86
Open: daily, 8pm–2am (4am Fri/Sat)

Le Duplex is a civilised slice of gay
Paris, more of a bar than a club, but
very much a party place at weekends.
An arty crowd of regulars come here
to chat and hang out to the sounds of
jazz and world music; it's a forum for
discussion and for contemporary art,
with changing monthly exhibitions of
mainly gay, male artists. There's room

to perch at high stools and tables near
the bar, with the rest of the floor kept
empty to accommodate the eventual
crowds. The upstairs room is comfortable and even homely, with brick walls
and leather club chairs, and a handy
view of the weekend dancers below.
Girls are welcome, but it's all about
boys here, really.

Favela Chic   *(bottom)*
18 rue Faubourg du
Temple, 11ème
Tel: 01 40 21 38 14
www.favelachic.com
Open: daily, 8pm–2am (4am Fri/Sat)

It could be argued that it's a bit thought-
less to name your disco after someone
else's rather trying living conditions, but
Favela Chic throws a decent party, and
bigs up Brazilian culture while it's at
it. It's not terribly chic, not by Parisian
standards, but it is a great place to go
for a dance when you've had your fill of
Oberkampf grunge. The cocktails are
effective, rather than sophisticated, and
the music formula is two parts Latin
and one part knowingly cheesy classics. Illuminated by upside-down lamps
and a disco ball, the crowd dress up to
party Brazilian-style and usually get
quite messy, in a whooping, caipirinha-
fuelled way. Expect queues as well as
an entrance fee on Friday and Saturday
nights, when the place is always kicking. The restaurant is strictly for fuel,
with its bright lights, and food that's
only OK; there's a sister establishment
in Shoreditch, with the same look but a
harder-edged music menu.

party...

Folie's Pigalle *(left)*
11 place Pigalle, 9ème
Tel: 01 48 78 55 25
www.folies-pigalle.com
Open: daily, midnight–6am (11am Sat/Sun)

You might not expect it from a striptease landmark with bordello trimmings in red 'n' gold, but Folie's Pigalle is dedicated to pumping house music, with just a sprinkling of other danceable genres. It gets hot and sticky on the dancefloor, only slightly less so on the air-conditioned balcony; the crowd is mixed, friendly and up for it, especially at the weekend, when the beats go on till a messy 11am. There have always been gay nights on here, and now there's the Sunday gay tea dance, for which you can drag up if you care to, and tranny cabaret in the evening.

Glaz'art *(bottom)*
7–15 avenue de la
Porte de la Villette, 19ème
Tel: 01 40 36 55 65
www.glazart.com
Open: 8pm–midnight Thurs; 6pm–6am Fri–Sat

Roots, psychedelia, post-rock, dubstep… Glaz'art is a concert venue and club on the outskirts of the centre that does the eclectic thing very well, attracting clubbers from all over Paris. It's a converted bus station, and the exterior ain't much, but inside it feels nice and homely, with armchairs and tables set around a big dancefloor. The club nights get packed and sweaty, with an outdoor terrace offering welcome respite on midsummer nights. As you'd expect on the edge of the *banlieue*, drinks are inexpensive and, in summer, the adjacent carpark is transformed into a beach, with five tons of sand, WiFi, world-food Sunday brunch, boules, 'expérimentations soniques' and free concerts. Fun before profit – it could be the Glaz'art motto.

Point Ephémère *(right)*
200 quai de Valmy, 10ème
Tel: 01 40 34 02 48
www.pointephemere.org
Open: daily, noon–2am Mon–Sat; 1–9pm Sun

Basically, Point Ephémère is a big concrete box by the canal where a lot of really cool things happen. It's very fringe, very 10th arrondissement, run by a collective whose mission is to reclaim disused industrial sites and inject creativity. This club/gallery/restaurant incorporates artists' studios, recording facilities, workshops and a dance studio. The passing hedonist is most likely to be lured in by the canalside bar and terrace for a summertime beer, and to hang out with local hipsters by night, when a devotedly open-minded music policy means no tripe, guaranteed. The former builder's merchant opened in 2004 as a temporary venue, hence the name. Happily, it has become a fixture.

party…

Queen *(top)*
102 avenue des
Champs-Elysées, 8ème
Tel: 08 92 70 73 30
www.queen.fr
Open: daily, 11.30pm–late

This used to be a trendy gay club, then a hasbeen gay club, now it's a classic gay club – you know how it goes… Immense in size, Queen entertains on three levels, all with accompanying bars, and there's a fiercely guarded VIP area (well, we are on the Champs Elysées). It's open through the week, with more themed nights introduced of late: Monday nights mean Disco Queen; there's electro and house on Tuesdays, Ladies' Night on Wednesday (take note, hen parties), and housey dancey action Thursday to Saturday. Overkitsch welcomes girls, boys and all sorts for its deliriously camp 1980s and 1990s dance-music fest on Sunday nights, when you could turn up wearing two sequins and a banana, and no one would laugh.

Le Régine *(middle)*
49 rue de Ponthieu, 8ème
Tel: 01 43 59 21 13
www.leregine.com
Open: 11pm–6am Tues–Sat

Hotter than hot since it was re-opened in autumn 2008 by the Paris nightlife mafia known as La Clique, this old-timer is pure fun, and worth the effort it takes to get in. It was formerly known as Chez Regine, named for the nightlife legend of the 1970s; its recent aspirations are demonstrated by the fact that it has an 'art director' as host

and, frequently, DJ. The music is ace, very danceable, patchy in a good way, swerving from Hot Chip to old French slowies; and the crowd is interestingly gorgeous and, from time to time, abandoned. It's a real *boîte de nuit,* a cramped, carpeted dive with a bar, a dancefloor and limited seating of the velvety-banquette kind. It fills up between 2am and 3am, with a good mix of slinky club kids and dubious night creatures.

Rex *(bottom)*
5 boulevard Poissonnière, 2ème
Tel: 01 42 36 10 96
www.rexclub.com
Open: daily, 11pm–6am

A real techno institution, Rex has been pumping out quality house music for some 20 years, steadily improving its sound system in order to continue attracting those superstar DJs. Laurent Garnier has been a regular for years, and the big names keep on coming: Sven Vath, Jeff Mills, Carl Cox. It's good for hearing what up-and-coming DJs are up to, too, with frequent label showcases and lots of international talent. Check out what's on in advance, rather than turning up excited, only to find you're there on one of the nights when it's a bit dead. On a good night, it's rocking: the space isn't as big as the music policy might suggest, but you can still put your hands in the air like you just don't care.

party…

ShowCase *(left)*

pont Alexandre III, 8ème
Tel: 01 45 61 25 43
www.showcase.fr
Open: 10pm–dawn Fri/Sat. (check
website during the week)

A massive, unique new nightlife space,
a former boat hangar beneath one of
the monumental stone arches of the
Alexandre III bridge, ShowCase is
thrilling at its best, owing to its sheer
size: there's room for 1,500 people in
its maw. It's perhaps not at its best
on a Saturday night, when swarms of
teenagers descend to dance and drink;
but if you find yourself invited to an af-
ter-party or to see an upcoming band
play there, it's impressive. The sound
system is knee-trembling, there's seating where over-25s can relax, and it's
surprisingly easy to get served at the
bar. It's also the sort of place you might
find yourself lured into, during a noc-
turnal riverside promenade; if you're
after a drink and a dance, you won't
be disappointed but, for sophisticated
night culture, keep walking.

Social Club *(bottom)*

142 rue Montmartre,
Grands Boulevards
Tel: 01 40 28 05 55
Open: 11pm–6am Thurs–Sat

The neon-lit discotheque formerly
known as Triptyque, Social Club has
been reincarnated as an, ahem, social
club for the nu-rave generation. A cool-
looking, friendly, daft-dancing crowd
piles onto the heaving dancefloor to
wiggle to Madonna, Prince and Bobby
Brown; there's seating down the other

end of the L-shaped basement, where
you can just about converse, or sit and
watch the parade of high-fiving youth.
In tune with the MySpace generation,
there are lots of electro nights, as well
as parties where you don't have to
queue if you come dressed as a su-
perhero. A great pitstop on the Grands
Boulevards nightlife trail, where you're
very likely to have lots of fun. Look out
for DJ sets from Simian Mobile Disco,
Scratch Perverts, and turns from the
likes of Afrika Bambaata and Grand-
master Flash.

Le Troisième Lieu *(right)*

62 rue Quincampoix, 4ème
Tel: 01 48 04 85 64
www.letroisiemelieu.com
Open: 6pm–6am (2am Thurs)
Thurs–Sat

Known for their I Hate Sundays tea
dance, the Ginettes Armées girls set
up this lesbian/mixed venue on two
floors as their permanent 'canteen'.
There's a welcoming, quasi-domestic
vibe: the ground floor's great for drinking, snacking and chatting; you can
perch at the long bar, settle in with a
beer at one of the Formica tables, or
head for the back room, decorated
with kitsch wallpaper and chandeliers.
Table football is a popular pastime,
early evening; later on, things liven up
downstairs, where grungey-cool girls
and boys dance to electro and minimal house; the Troisième Lieu family
includes the record shop next door, My
Electro Kitchen.

party...

Le VIP Room *(top)*

188 rue de Rivoli, 1er
Tel: 01 58 36 46 00 www.viproom.fr
Open: midnight–5am. Closed Mondays.

With its resoundingly unironic name, and sibling establishments in St Tropez and Cannes, the VIP Room's status can be in no doubt. It's a Dom Pérignon-pouring, podium-dancing, supermodel-friendly kinda place, with a music policy of up-for-it house and garage, and blingy hip-hop. Karl Lagerfeld has been seen to enjoy himself here, and it's a natural habitat for P Diddy, Paris Hilton, French celebs and people you see in *Hello!* It moved recently from the Champs Elysées, but little has changed: the decor is luxy-disco, the dress code's expensive and flimsy, and the champagne always flows. N.B.: it's pronounced 'vip', to rhyme with 'who's got the keys to my Jeep'.

....

Wagg *(bottom)*

62 rue Mazarine, 6ème
Tel: 01 55 42 22 01 www.wagg.fr
Open: 11.30pm–6am Fri/Sat;
3pm–midnight Sun

Once the Whisky A Go-Go, where Jim Morrison may have spent his last night (there are a few enshrined psychedelic relics, such as a groovy painted door in the corridor), the WAGG attracted star DJs in the 1990s, but now caters for an unpretentious mainstream demographic. It's geared towards dancing and group fun, with a dancefloor surrounded by booths with tables and couches, and a long bar. Every Friday, WAGG is home to a fine British import, the evergreen 1970s funk night Carwash, when flares and afro wigs take over. Other regular nights include Fade To Grey (not a 1980s night, but house and garage), and Golden 80s (that's more like it). All in all, an undemanding place to come for a dance when you're not feeling übercool.

....

LIVE MUSIC

L'Attirail

9 rue au Maire, 3ème
Tel: 01 42 72 44 42
www.lattirail.com
Open: daily, midnight–2am

A small and authentic venue in the Chinese quarter, L'Attirail is run by a pair of Algerian-born brothers, who book in different bands and performers nightly, to play klezmer, gypsy music, swing or chanson. The walls of the bar are plastered with peeling posters and photographs of musicians, and you can expect to mingle with a young, cool crowd. There's a short menu of salads, *confit de canard* and steaks.; happy hour, from 3.30pm to 7.30pm daily, simply means €2 pastis.

....

Le Baiser Salé

58 rue des Lombards, 1er
Tel: 01 42 33 37 71
www.lebaisersale.com
Bar open: daily, 5.30pm–6am.
Concerts daily, 7pm and 10pm

The 'salty kiss' has been tooting and parping for some 25 years, providing a space for jazz in all its hybrid forms, so you might come across an all-star funk ensemble, a Cuban flute jam,

party…

Cape Verdean saudade blues, or an afro-jazz festival. There's a horseshoe bar where musicians and regulars hang out till late, enjoying the mellow, appealingly seedy atmosphere. The cocktails aren't prize-winners but the music programming shouldn't disappoint.

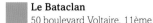

Le Bataclan
50 boulevard Voltaire, 11ème
Tel: 01 43 14 00 30
www.le-bataclan.com
Open: daily, 11.30pm–6am

A Paris institution, dating back to 1864, Le Bataclan has seen 'em all, booking in the best mainstream-to-edgy rock, hip-hop and pop acts. At the time of going to press, upcoming shows include La Roux, Hot Chip, the Stranglers and Yo La Tengo; Lou Reed has a live album named after it. There are club nights here at weekends, too, with the converted theatre space providing a huge dancefloor.

Chez Adel
10 rue de la
Grange-aux-Belles, 10ème
Tel: 01 42 08 24 61
Open: noon–midnight. Closed Mondays.

Presided over by the eponymous owner, this rootsy little place just off the Canal St-Martin is a great place to hear *chanson française*.

La Cigale
120 bvd de
Rochechouart, 18ème
Tel 01 49 25 81 75
www.lacigale.fr
Open: daily, 7.30pm–whenever gigs end

A listed theatre where Arletty and Mistinguett performed and Cocteau got surreal, La Cigale was reopened at the end of the 1980s as a cultish rock and pop venue, hosting edgier French and international acts. If you want to catch the likes of Animal Collective, Devendra Banhart or Bonnie Prince Billy, this is a great, atmospheric venue, with two bars and numbered seating.

Le Gambetta
104 rue Bagnolet, 20ème
Tel: 01 43 70 52 01
www.gambetta-bar.com
Open: daily, 10am–2am

A rocking little hang-out hosting reggae, rai and funk parties, with live acts several evenings a week and DJs nightly: when the bands have finished playing, the sound system kicks in, and official opening hours are elastic, depending on collective enthusiasm. Beers include Mort Subite and Pelforth Blonde, with prices increasing as the night goes by.

La Maroquinerie
23 rue Boyer, 20ème
Tel: 01 40 33 35 05
www.lamaroquinerie.fr
Gigs: 8pm Mon–Fri

Great up-and-coming bands are the chief draw of Le Maroquinerie: Anglo acts like Bon Iver, Speech Debelle and Cornershop, the Inrocks Indie Club night, and a smattering of the world music that used to be its mainstay. There's a bar and restaurant, the former good for hooking up before a gig, the latter only recommended if you're in need of fuel.

La Mécanique Ondulatoire
8 passage Thière, 11ème
www.lamecond.com
Open: 6pm–2am. Closed Sundays.

A relative newcomer to the Bastille scene, this is a rock/indie/electro hang-out on three levels, with a concert hall in the vaulted cellar, huge ground-floor bar and gallery space upstairs, devoted to photography exhibitions. The decor is quirky and retro, in a new-wave kinda way, and beers and mojitos are easy on the pocket.

Nouveau Casino
109 rue Oberkampf, 11ème
Tel: 01 43 57 57 40
www.nouveaucasino.net
Open: daily, midnight–6am (gigs start at 7pm – check website for listings)

Next door to Café Charbon (see Drink), the doyen of Oberkampf bars, Le Nouveau Casino is a busy mainstream venue and club in a former factory space, with a red-lit fibreglass bar contrasting with the stark industrial interior. Bands come on at 7pm, followed by club nights Thursday to Saturday; the talent is largely pop/rock/hip-hop, with recent appearances from Joan As Police Woman, Glasvegas and Dans Le Sac vs Scroobius Pip.

La Scène Bastille
2 bis rue des Taillandiers, 11ème
Tel: 01 48 06 50 70
www.scenebastille.com
Open: daily, 7.30pm till 11pm for concerts, midnight–6am for clubbing

There's a big dancefloor at this central venue and club, where live acts (reggae, hip-hop, metal, acoustic) are followed by rammed club nights (disco, reggaeton, lots of techno). When it all gets a bit sweaty, there's also a chill-out room and various alcoves to drink and chat in.

party...

SEXY TIME

Swinging is alive and well in Paris, and not just in the suburbs… There are numerous *échangiste* clubs, varying gently in terms of client pulchritude and degree of dressing up, fetish or otherwise. They are usually rather civilised, aimed at couples (single women get in free), and with buffets and drinks served. Illicit venues are known as *clubs*, with normal nightclubs referred to as *boîtes de nuit*. Brothel bars, which proliferate around Place Pigalle, are tolerated by the law; prostitution itself is not illegal in Paris (pimping and soliciting are), though there's plenty of action around St-Denis, Pigalle and Clichy, and cross-dressing *travesties* lurking in the Bois de Boulogne.

STRIP CLUBS

Pink Paradise
49–51 rue de Ponthieu, 8ème
Tel: 01 58 36 19 20
www.pinkparadise.fr

Paris' first lap-dancing club, an upmarket venue with VIP rooms, located on a toney nightlife strip, and owned by DJ and promoter David Guetta and his wife Cathy.

Hustler Club Paris
13–15 rue de Berri, 8ème
Tel: 01 53 53 86 00
www.hustlerclubparis.com

Lap dancing and table dancing, American-style, courtesy of Larry Flynt.

SWINGERS' CLUBS

Les Chandelles
1 rue Thérèse, 1èr
Tel: 01 42 60 43 31
www.les-chandelles.com

Chi-chi club for couples, with an emphasis on aesthetics. Check out the reading list on the website, which runs from *intello* French sex guides to *Les Fleurs du Mal* – nice! Single men allowed till 9pm, and all night on Monday.

L'Overside
92 rue du Cherche-midi, 6ème
Tel: 01 42 84 10 20
www.overside.fr

Left Bank sex club with a disco and various *salons* to allow voyeurism, group adventures or a little light bondage. Single men allowed Wednesdays and Sundays.

Le Roi René
184 rue de Versailles,
Ville d'Avray
Tel: 01 47 09 22 27
www.roi-rene.com

Historic libertines' hang-out, in the western suburbs, with decadent decor and a professional clientele.

Chateau des Lys
103 rue Marcadet, 18ème
Tel: 01 42 58 13 01
www.chateauclub.fr

A swingers' club near Montmartre,

Le VIP Room

party...

hosting lots of events and themed nights. Strictly couples only on Friday and Saturday nights.

FETISH CLUBS

 **Cris et Chuchautements**
9 rue Truffaut, 17ème
Tel: 01 42 93 70 21
www.cris-et-chuchotements.com

A stylish Montmartre S&M club, complete with racks, restraints, and so on, which puts on nights such as 'Piano and strings', with a musician and bond-age experts, and 'Japan Eros', with sushi and green tea.

La Nuit Elastique
www.nuit-elastique.com

Club promotions with a strict rubber/vinyl/leather/latex dress code, in venues around the city, including river boats and the dungeonesque Caves le Chapelais near Place de Clichy.

culture...

There's a great deal to be said for a certain degree of intellectual snobbery. Parisians take their culture seriously – not just as collective custodians of more than 1,800 classified monuments, 170 museums, 145 theatres and 380 cinemas, but also as producers and consumers of new stuff, whether it's highbrow or hip-hop. That means there's no danger of this incredible city feeling like a heritage trail; rather, there's always a new arts space, wacky collaboration, publicly funded bright idea or underground happening to seek out.

2009 saw the opening of two new arts centres: 104, a reclaimed municipal building in Montmartre, where 16 resident international artists work freely on interactive projects; and the bright-green, architecturally fluid Cité de la Mode et du Dessin, likewise offering up restaurants, cafés, a club and retail thrills alongside arty/educational elements. Other recent additions to the cultural scene are L'Espace Claude Berri, a Marais showcase for the contemporary collection of film-maker Berri; and Le Palace, the famed former nightclub (and squat), which has reopened as a swish theatre.

So, where to start? With a stroll. A wholesome, outdoorsy way to encounter the city's cultural heroes is to take a wander round either of its best-loved cemeteries – Père-Lachaise and Montparnasse – where you can ponder the greatness of everyone from Frédéric Chopin and Charles Baudelaire to Sam Beckett and Serge Gainsbourg.

Once you've enjoyed a bit of *flânerie* among the dead, you'll be ready for some life-affirming art. The Louvre is best experienced as a lifelong sequence of short visits, unless you think you're hard enough to check out all 35,000 artworks and artefacts at once... The Musée d'Orsay is, perhaps, easier to love, and *the* place for Impressionists, though Musée Marmottan in the 16th is home to more Monets (and his Water Lilies are on show at the Musée de l'Orangerie, in the Tuileries gardens).

Three major institutions are devoted to decorative arts: the Musée des Arts Decoratifs, in the west wing of the Louvre; the Galerie des Gobelins, in the 13th; and Le Petit Palais. Smaller and perhaps even more of a pleasure to visit are the smaller museums. The Musée Rodin, Musée Gustave-Moreau, Musée Carnava-

Eiffel Tower

Louvre

*Maison Européene
de la Photgraphie*

let and Musée de la Vie Romantique are refined, romantic favourites; Yves Saint Laurent, Le Corbusier, Edith Piaf and Honoré de Balzac all have sites devoted to them.

Contemporary art biggies are the Centre Pompidou, the Palais de Tokyo and the Jeu de Paume, which is tops for photography, along with the Maison Européenne de la Photographie and Fondation Henri Cartier-Bresson. Finally, the controversial Musée du Quai Branly, designed by Jean Nouvel and inaugurated in 2006, houses art and artefacts from Africa, Asia and Oceania.

Film buffs are definitely in the right city: multiplex isn't a dirty word in Paris, where art-house and international pictures are shown at big complexes alongside mainstream fare. This means the art-house cinemas themselves can get really obscure, with weird documentaries, retrospectives and culter-than-cult flicks. On rue des Écoles in the Latin Quarter, Grand Action and Champo have been going since the New Wave was news; Accatone used to be managed by François Truffaut. Studio 28, which featured in *Amélie*, was a haunt of Jean Cocteau; other historic beauties are La Pagode, built in 1896; and massive Le Grand Rex, an art deco multiplex.

Performing arts are well funded and well fed with young talent; even the ultra-venerable Comédie Française puts on new work alongside its classical repertoire. There's world-class opera and ballet at the Opéra Garnier and Opéra Bastille; and classical-music performances at Salle Pleyel (resident bands: Orchestre de Paris, London Symphony Orchestra) and Châtelet – Théâtre Musical de Paris, whose programming is a bit more eclectic. Popwise, stadium acts perform at the Olympia, Bercy or Zénith; up-and-coming bands play at venues such as La Bataclan and Elysée Montmartre. Whatever your thing – jazz, world, chanson, cabaret, indie-rock – you're guaranteed to get your kicks.

Among mayor Bertrand Delanoë's cultural coups is the yearly Nuit Blanche in October, when dozens of museums, galleries and temporary art spaces (churches, swimming pools…) are open right through the night. Other festivals of note are the Fête de la Musique in June, Jazz à la Villette in September, the Festival d'Automne and Les Inrockuptibles in November. You might also like a bit of Cinéma en Plein Air at Parc de la Villette, July–August.

SIGHTSEEING

■ **Cimetière du** *(left)*
■ **Montparnasse**

3 boulevard Edgar-Quinet, 14ème
Tel: 01 44 10 86 50
Open: daily, 8am to 9.30am opening,
5.30pm to 6.30pm closing, depending
on day and time of year

Not as starry as Père-Lachaise, but
more peaceful (no Jim Morrison nec-
rophiles) and the eternal resting place
of more left-field writers, artists and
thinkers. Spend a sunny Sunday afternoon wandering its 1,800 acres and
you can pay your respects to Man Ray,
Jean Baudrillard, Tristan Tzara, Simone
de Beauvoir and Jean-Paul Sartre, and
Susan Sontag. The rock-star pilgrimage here is Serge Gainsbourg, whose
grave is always festooned with love
notes, Gitanes cigarettes and bottles
of booze.

■ **Cimetière du** *(right)*
■ **Père-Lachaise**

Boulevard de Ménilmontant, 20ème
Tel: 01 55 25 82 10
www.pere-lachaise.com
Open: daily, 8am to 9.30am opening,
5.30pm to 6.30pm closing, depending
on day and time of year

Père-Lachaise is just wonderful, a me-
andering, gothic fairyland of monuments grand and grotesque, and so vast
you could spend days trying to orient
yourself. It was established in the late
1700s, when the city's graveyards were
getting a bit full, and became 'fashionable' once the remains of Molière and
La Fontaine were deployed as bait. The
graves are sold with varying degrees

of permanence, from 10-year leases
to perpetuity; there are lots of non-
famous people interred here, but also
hundreds of famous writers, compos-
ers, statesmen, actors and aristocrats.
Apart from Jim Morrison's grave,
which is now patrolled to prevent acts
of bad taste, the ones that provoke the
most excitement are those of Oscar
Wilde, Marcel Proust and one Victor
Noir, whose prominently groined like-
ness has achieved shiny fertility-object
status. Good luck trying to find any of
them – maps are on sale at the main
entrance (weekdays only).

■ **Eiffel Tower** *(bottom)*
■ Champs de Mars, 7ème

Tel: 01 44 11 23 45
www.tour-eiffel.fr
Open: daily, 9am–12.45am mid-
June–mid-Sept; 9.30am–11.45pm
mid-Sept–mid-June

Built as a temporary emblem for the
1889 International Exhibition, the Eiffel Tower has become *the* iconic landmark of the French capital, though its
radical design was loudly criticised at
the time of construction. Standing 324
metres high, the puddle-iron structure
was the world's tallest building until 1930, and still gives super-duper
views of Paris. It's divided into three
accessible platforms, the first and second levels reached either pounding up
the stairs or via one of three lifts, the
third connected by lift from the second floor. There are several queues to
conquer: one to buy your ticket, one
to reach the first or second floor, and
– the longest and most painful – one
for the top. In addition to the view,
you get lots of historical, interactive,

multilingual video whatnots, and kiosks selling snacks and souvenirs. Of the two restaurants, Le Jules Verne, on the second level, has been under the direction of Alain Ducasse since 2007 and is, correspondingly, well-nigh impossible to get a table at (see Eat).

Institut du *(left)*
Monde Arabe
1 rue des Fossés-St –Bernard, 5ème
Tel: 01 40 51 38 38
www.imarabe.org
Museum open: daily, 10am–6pm.
Closed Sundays. Library open: 1–8pm.
Closed Sundays and Mondays.

The geometric motifs covering the south façade of Jean Nouvel's Seine-side cultural centre double as high-tech automated apertures that control the amount of sunlight entering the building – a method of filtering light into the interior that was inspired by Moorish ingenuity. Within is a museum, illuminating the history and archaeology of the Arab/Islamic world, with displays of calligraphy, decorative arts, miniatures and photography. Other draws are the superlative Middle East bookshop, sweeping city views from the roof terrace (admission is free to both of these), and regular blockbuster exhibitions. There are guided tours at 3pm during the week, and 4.30pm Saturdays and Sundays.

Mémorial des *(right)*
Martyrs de La Déportation
Square de l'Ile de France, 4ème
Tel: 01 46 33 87 56
Open: daily, 10am–noon, 2–7pm Apr–Sept; 10am–noon, 2–5pm Oct–Mar

At the eastern tip of the Ile de la Cité, down a couple of steps, is a well-hidden memorial dedicated to the memory of those deported from France to German concentration camps during World War II. Simple chambers are lined with 200,000 lights representing the 200,000 individuals who died at the hands of the Nazis. The 1960s design manages to be both beautiful and bleak; a barred window looks out to the Seine, and poetry engraved on the walls invites a moment of reflection.

ART GALLERIES

Louvre *(bottom)*
Cours Napoleon, 1er
Tel: 01 40 20 50 50
www.louvre.fr
Open: 9am–6pm (10pm Wed, Fri).
Closed Tuesdays.

Set in Louis XIV's palace, with the magnificent Tuileries as its back garden, and housing around 35,000 works of art, this overwhelmingly pre-eminent museum demands a planned visit, so decide in advance what you would like to see, buy your tickets online and avoid the queues. The main entrance is through I.M. Pei's thrilling glass and steel pyramid in the Cour Napoléon, but advance-ticket holders can enter via the passage Richelieu from rue de Rivoli. Inside, the huge collection includes European art from the Middle Ages to the mid-19th century, artefacts from the Islamic world, Egypt and Rome, decorative arts and sculpture. Among the superstar moments are the world's most famous painting, the Mona Lisa, known as La Joconde in French; Gericault's apocalyptic

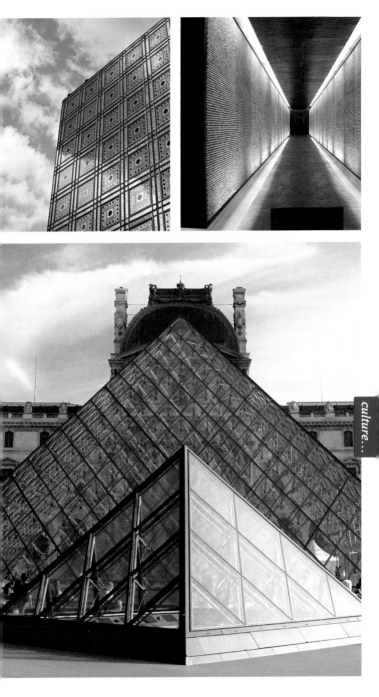

culture...

La Radeau de la Méduse; and Liberty Leading the People by Delacroix. Don't miss the Michelangelo and Donatello sculptures, the amazing Titians on the rear of the mobbed Mona Lisa, nor Cranach's Anne of Cleves. When it all gets too much, escape to Café Marly (see Snack) or Le Fumoir (see Eat). On top of the permanent collections, the Louvre puts on regular blockbuster shows; and concerts and so on take place in the 450-seat auditorium located beneath the pyramid.

Musée National Gustave-Moreau *(left)*

14 rue de La Rochefoucauld, 9ème
Tel: 01 48 74 38 50
www.musee-moreau.fr
Open: 10am–12.45pm, 2–5.15pm.
Closed Tuesdays.

This quirky, fascinating place is a 19th-century timewarp, a private home conceived as a museum by the artist owner himself before he died in 1898. Symbolist painter Gustave Moreau bequeathed his house and art collection (not to mention his cabinet of curiosities) to the state, on the condition it was left untouched, preserving his legacy and underscoring his eccentricities for posterity. As well as his masterpieces – fantastical canvases featuring mythological and biblical scenes – you'll see rare books, drawings, family portraits and a collection of Grand Tour souvenirs. On the upper floor is a rotating display case for watercolours, designed to Moreau's specifications; the museum is laid out to allow visitors to see as many of the 4,800 drawings and 450 watercolours as possible. The artist's private apartments are just as crammed with objets, paintings and original furniture.

Musée d'Orsay *(right)*

62 rue de Lille, 7ème
Tel: 01 40 49 48 14
www.musee-orsay.fr
Open: 9.30am–6pm (9.45pm Thurs).
Closed Mondays.

Behold Impressionists galore in this beautiful turn-of-the-century railway station on the Left Bank, as well as major examples of Post-Impressionism, Symbolism, Romanticism, Pointillism and Neoclassicism. The vast interior contains a chronological cornucopia of works by Manet, Monet, Renoir, Degas, Cézanne, Corot, Courbet, Gauguin and Van Gogh, plus sculpture and decorative arts; the collections cover the period from 1848 to 1914, with art nouveau well represented (Lalique, Klimt) and sections devoted to architectural drawings and early photography. Manet's Olympia and his groundbreaking Déjeuner sur l'Herbe are both here, along with sensual, exotic Gauguins, the nightlife art of Toulouse-Lautrec, and dreamlike pastels by Odilon Redon. Don't be ashamed of spending some quality time in the bookshop; there are also two cafés and a restaurant.

Musée Rodin *(bottom)*

79 rue de Varenne, 7ème
Tel: 01 44 18 61 10
www.musee-rodin.fr
Open: daily, 9.30am–5.45pm Apr–Sept;
9.30am–4.45pm Oct–Mar

The Rodin Museum is set in a superb

culture...

hôtel particulier, which has housed nuns, artists and dancers since it was built in 1728. It is now one of the most charming museums in Paris, dedicated to the life and work of Auguste Rodin, with a permanent collection that includes The Kiss, The Thinker, The Walking Man, many terracotta busts and figures, and thousands of drawings and prints. Rodin's work is accompanied by a number of pieces by his mistress and pupil Camille Claudel; among the artwork he donated to the state before his death are paintings by Van Gogh, Renoir and Monet. There are more epoch-making sculptures in the gardens, which are indescribably romantic.

CONTEMPORARY ART

104 *(left)*
104 rue d'Aubervilliers, 19ème
Tel: 01 53 35 50 00
ww.104.fr
Open: daily, 11am–11pm (8pm Sun/Mon)

Backed by Mayor Delanoë and intended to break down boundaries between art producers and public, 'Le Cent Quatre' is one of those very French institutions that combines an avowedly non-elitist approach with intelligent programming. Artists from all over the world are invited to develop and show their work in the 16 workshop spaces, and offered all-round support, in return for a willingness to open up the creative process to involve viewers. The 15,000 sq/m complex, a 19th-century municipal behemoth in the 19th arrondissement, also has a café and pizza truck, an inexpensive restaurant, due to open in 2010, a dedicated House of Children (like a creative indoor playground), a bookshop and a concept store for pop-up retail action.

Centre Georges Pompidou *(right)*
rue St-Martin, 4ème
Tel: 01 44 78 12 33
www.centrepompidou.fr
Open: 11am–9pm (11pm Thurs). Closed Tuesdays.

Beaubourg, as it is usually known, was designed by Renzo Piano and Richard Rogers (then celebrities-to-be) and completed in 1977. The high-tech structure, with its mechanical elements externalised via bright tubes and ducts (colour-coded, fact fans), houses the national collection of modern art, a public library, plus cinema, performance and exhibition spaces, and Georges restaurant (see Eat). There's a partial rehang each year, and regular retrospectives and themed shows: Alexander Calder and Kandinski in 2009; an all-women blockbuster in 2010. A quick how-to: buy your tickets on the ground floor, then head up to level four to see art since 1960, and level five for 1905–1960.

Palais de Tokyo *(bottom)*
13 avenue de Président-Wilson, 16ème
Tel: 01 47 23 54 01
www.palaisdetokyo.com
Open: noon–midnight. Closed Mondays.

Don't be confused by the name; this isn't a museum dedicated to Japan, but a showcase for contemporary art. People just got into the habit of calling the building the Palais de Tokyo, because the riverbank below was known as the quai de Tokyo. Built for the International Exposition of Arts and Techniques of 1937, it housed Paris' National Museum of Modern Art before that moved to the Centre Georges Pompidou. Since it was reincarnated as a centre for contemporary art in 2002, curators Nicolas Bourriaud and Jérôme Sans have been putting together a challenging mix of cross-disciplinary media in a gutted, blank-canvas space; there are also four cinema screens dedicated to experimental and art-house film. The groovy opening hours, along with a trendy restaurant, café and shops, pull in a cool, young urban crowd.

PHOTOGRAPHY

Le Jeu de Paume *(top)*
1 place de la Concorde, 8ème
Tel: 01 47 03 12 50
www.jeudepaume.org
Open: daily, noon (10am Sat/Sun)–7pm (9pm Tues)

This central exhibition space for photography and video art has been home since 2005 to the Centre National de la Photographie. It's an historic site, a former real tennis court, not that that distracts from the retrospectives and one-man shows (Cindy Sherman, Martin Parr). Some exhibitions travel over from museums such as MoMA in New York; international video and digital artists are shown downstairs in the video-art and cinema suite. The bookshop is irresistibly authoritative. There's a twin site at the Hôtel de Sully in the Bastille (62 rue Saint-Antoine, tel: 01 42 74 47 75).

Maison Européenne *(bottom)*
de la Photographie
5–7 rue de Fourcy, 4ème
Tel: 01 44 78 75 00 www.mep-fr.org
Open: 11am–8pm. Closed Mondays and Tuesdays.

Occupying a renovated and extended 17th-century mansion, the Maison Européenne de la Photographie is probably the number-one photography gallery and exhibition space in the city, owing to its amazing 15,000-strong collections alone. The space is spread over three floors and comprises an exhibition centre, library and auditorium, as well as a bookshop and café. All styles, from reportage to fashion photography, are well represented; the last few years have seen shows on Martin Parr, Orlan, China, Jean Baudrillard, William Klein, Annie Leibowitz and Henri Cartier-Bresson, usually accompanied by film screenings and/or publications. The MEP also organises the biennial Mois de la Photo festival, taking place in 2010 and 2012.

MAISON EUROPEENNE DE
LA PHOTOGRAPHIE
VILLE DE PARIS

OPERA/BALLET

Opéra Bastille *(top)*
Place de la Bastille, 12ème
Tel: 01 72 29 35 35
www.operadeparis.fr

A thoroughly modern counterpart to the wedding-cake exuberance of Opéra Garnier, this is one of Mitterand's *grands projets*, inaugurated in 1989 on the 200th anniversary of the storming of the Bastille prison. The high-tech architecture is more derided than loved, and the acoustics are famously tricky, but the Opéra National de Paris productions are world-class, and star turns by top international artists are a given. Every one of the 2,273 seats in the main auditorium is meant to have an unimpeded view of the stage, and ticket prices can be anything from €5 (standing) to €175. The standing tickets go on sale daily, 90 minutes before the curtain rises. The programme includes Die Walküre, Billy Budd and The Cunning Little Vixen.

Opéra Garnier *(bottom)*
Place de l'Opéra, 9ème
Tel: 01 72 29 35 35
www.operadeparis.fr

This smaller but more magnificent neo-baroque edifice, built by Charles Garnier in the 1860s, drips with statuary and friezes, its interior all gold leaf, red velvet and cherubs; the whopping chandelier weighs six tons, and the gorgeous ceiling was painted by Marc Chagall in 1964. It can accommodate the most extravagant performances, with a stage big enough for 450 performers, and revolving machinery that can carry running horses. The underground lake and cellars inspired Gaston Leroux to write The Phantom of the Opera; in real life the lake was a bind for the builders, with eight months of day-and-night pumping required before the show could go on. Opera and ballet performances here often sell out weeks in advance but, as at Opéra Bastille, there are day tickets available if you're determined. Visiting conductors include Emmanuelle Haïm and Marc Minkowksi.

THEATRE

La Comédie Française
Salle Richelieu,
2 rue Richelieu, 1er
Tel: 01 44 58 15 15
www.comedie-francaise.fr

Founded in 1680 and associated with the works of Molière, Racine and Corneille, the venerable Comédie Française has three sites: the velvety Salle Richelieu on the Place Colette in the 1er; the Théâtre du Vieux-Colombier in the 6ème; and the Studio-Théâtre beneath IM Pei's glittering pyramid in the Louvre. Uniquely, this is a state theatre with its own troupe of actors and a repertoire of some 3,000 plays, from Plato's Symposium, via an overwhelming majority of classical dramas, to Alfred Jarry's Ubu Roi. Excellent new productions are mounted regularly, such as the 2009/2010 season's La Grande Magie by Eduardo di Filippo, directed by Brit Dan Jemmett.

culture...

CINEMA

Le Grand Rex *(top)*
1 boulevard Poissonnière, 2ème
Tel: 08 92 68 05 96
www.legrandrex.com

This enormous cinema wasn't named Le 'Grand' Rex for nothing and, more than 60 years after launch, it is still Paris's biggest picture house. Its plush baroque-style interior and art deco façade make it a must for cinema enthusiasts who appreciate a spot of old-school grandeur. Sitting on the high-level red velvet seats is such a worthwhile experience, it barely matters whether or not you can understand the dialogue though, if you're lucky, you'll be able to catch an Anglophone film with French subtitles (look out for the 'VO' symbol, standing for Version Original). Don't come expecting a bill of vintage fare to match the fairytale looks; this is a mainstream multiplex, effectively, with six smaller screens, all leaning towards blockbusters. Look out for festivals, seasons and after-dark events.

Studio 28 *(bottom)*
10 rue Tholozé, 18ème
Tel: 01 46 06 36 07
www.cinemastudio28.com

Montmartre's creative crowd watch art-house and classic films at this retro cinema, which has remained largely unchanged since it first opened in the 1920s (except that, thanks to government funding, it now has an *haut-def* projector and spotless screen with Dolby surround sound). It was an essential meeting place for avant-garde film-makers: Luis Buñuel first aired L'Age d'Or here, and Jean Cocteau even designed the light-fittings. More recently, it played a supporting role in feelgood hit Amélie. Meet before the movie for drinks at the tiny foyer bar, or find a perch in the covered courtyard café, though it gets very busy at the weekends.

shop...

The pleasure of shopping in Paris was always very much about the rituals and idiosyncrasies of the specialist retailer. Scent, umbrellas, lingerie and gloves all continue to be sold in small boutiques, with some *quartiers* retaining their historic connection with, say, books (5th arrondissement) or antiques (7th arrondissement). If old-school experts are becoming rarities, a newer trend is sustaining the Parisian sense of expertise and authenticity: the rise of independent fashion boutiques whose buyers (often the owners) are creative, passionate and supportive of emerging talent.

The original Paris concept store – that is, an edgy-ish fashion shop that sells art books and mags, design, sometimes furniture, as well as accessories – was and is Colette, still going strong at 213 rue Saint-Honoré and now a fixture on the tourist trail. L'Eclaireur is less pop, more intriguing; ultra-respected Maria Luisa focuses on fashion labels. The effect is that of a kind of lifestyle primer for the consumer and, for the small brand, a big break. The new generation of concept/multibrand boutiques include AB33, Shine and Surface to Air in the Haut-Marais, and Spree and No Good Store in Montmartre.

The 'Golden Triangle' on the Right Bank is unchallenged as the heartland of the city's fashion industry, where the legends do business. Chanel, Dior, Hermès, Louis Vuitton – each has to have its high-status shopfront on or around the Avenue de Montaigne, Avenue Georges V and the Champs-Elysées. Even these have been influenced by creativity of the lifestyle fashion boutiques, bringing contemporary art instore (Louis Vuitton) or revamping their interiors to convey a unique style; just before the recession hit, Givenchy, Lanvin, Yves Saint Laurent and Sonia Rykiel all lashed out on redesigns with wow factor.

The Champs-Elysées is, overwhelmingly, a high-street (and hectic) experience, although the new Le66 and rethought Drugstore Publicis are fun, and lots of shops are open late and on Sundays. The smartest shopping is on Rue Saint-Honoré in the 1st arrondissement and its continuation in the 8eme, the Rue du Faubourg-St-Honoré. Also in the 1er, Place Vendôme is home to jewellers such as Cartier, Chaumet and their elite competitors. Le Palais Royal is a 'new' fashion quartier, anointed by Marc Jacobs, Rick Owens and Acne Jeans. The Montorgueil area, around Rue Etienne-Marcel and Rue Tiquetonne, still sees some bona fide rag-trade activity, but also increasing bobo gentrification and the contemporary fashion boutiques that come with it.

shop...

The 6th arrondissement has its fair share of upmarket and/or hip fashion outlets, though its narrower, winding streets are also full of dozens of antiques shops, bookstores and galleries; the main action is on Boulevard St-Germain and the narrow lanes running off it to Rue de Vaugirard; for shoes, the Rue de Grenelle is hard to beat. In the Marais, the Rue de Rosiers and Rue des Francs-Bourgeois still have a lot to offer, not least L'Eclaireur but, if you've been there and done that, head to the Haut-Marais, where hot designers and new stores have transformed Rues Charlot, Poitou and Saintonge into a hip destination. Montmartre just keeps getting trendier, so there's always something new to discover; the Place des Abbesses is a good starting place for a stroll with shopping intent.

Vintage boutiques abound in Paris, often selling classic or 1970s/1980s finds alongside original designs. For a vintage-oriented personal-shopper service, see www.oohlalavintage.com. The fleamarkets or *puces*, apart from being a classic Paris thing to do, are a great source of second-hand everything, from obscure junk to expensive, sought-after design pieces. We've only named a couple of food markets here, but every quartier has its own, from fancy-pants Marché Raspail in the 6ème to rootsy Marché Beauvais in the 12ème. Fabulous bakeries, pâtisseries, chocolatiers, fromageries, traiteurs and wine merchants are everywhere, and finding your own favourite is all part of the fun. Notable foodie streets are the Rue des Martyrs in the 19ème, where locals queue for bread and macaroons at Arnaud Delmontel bakery; Rue de Buci in St-Germain; and Rue Mouffetard in the 5ème.

Of 140 pre-Haussmann arcades – prototype malls, as critiqued by Walter Benjamin and surrealised by Louis Aragon – 30 remain, in various states of repair. Psychogeographers should make a pilgrimage to Passage Jouffroy, 9ème, or Passage des Panoramas, 2ème, to admire the glass roofs and elegant ironwork. Their modern-day counterpart, the department store, is represented in Paris by Le Bon Marché, Galeries Lafayette and Printemps; competition is fierce, not just between the three, but with the independent boutiques. One last pointer: we find that the staff in concept store beat hotel concierges hands-down when it comes to advice on new places to eat, drink and party.

General info: shops are open, generally speaking, between 10am and 7pm, with some boutiques still closing for lunch. Sunday opening is largely confined to the Marais and the Champs-Elysées; some smaller shops close for all or part of Monday, too. The department stores open late on Thursday, and lots of doors on the Champs-Elysées stay open till midnight.

Louvre & Palais Royal

Rue Cambon, 1er

Alice Cadolle (4) luxury lingerie from the legendary fifth-generation corset-makers

Costume National (5) Milan-based designers specialising in streamlined, rock-star garb for men and women

Fifi Chachnil (26) beautifully silky, saucy underwear

Chanel (29) haute-couture house synonymous with Paris. Coco's first boutique was at no 21. Also at 42 avenue Montaigne, 8ème.

Rue Saint-Honoré, 1er

Astier de Villatte (173) beautiful white ceramics and covetable scented candles – but the rustic premises are the best bit

Colette (213) the original Paris concept store is a fixture on the sightseeing route, with some Japanese tourists getting a cab there direct from Charles de Gaulle. The cherry-picked fashion, scent and gadgets are always impeccably hip and niche.

Miu Miu (219) Mrs Prada's second line. Also at 16 rue de Grenelle, 2ème

Paule Ka (223) modern, couture-influenced classics for women, with branches in the 4th, 6th and 8th arrondissements

Goyard (233) amazing handmade French luggage for big spenders

Minapoe (382) adored accessories store, now also selling eveningwear and cashmere

Jardins du Palais Royal, 1er

Didier Ludot (20 and 34 galerie de Montpensier) vintage haute couture of unimpeachable quality: Balenciaga, Dior, Balmain, Chanel...

Marc Jacobs (56–62 galerie de Montpensier) an ultra-elegant showroom for MJ's wares. His other Paris store is at 19 place du Marché Saint Honoré.

Martin Margiela (23 & 25 bis, rue de Montpensier) see Rue de Grenelle, below

Kitsuné 52 rue de Richelieu French/Japanese record label/fashion store/all-round hotbed of international, collaborative creativity

Stella McCartney (114–121 galerie de Valois) Ms Macca's first Paris outlet

Acne (124 galerie de Valois) ultra-cool Swedish jeanswear label

Rick Owens (130–133 galerie de Valois) the go-to designer for 21st-century louche, hooded, zipped and slim-fitting

Corto Moltedo (146-148 galerie de Valois) high-status handbags that mix traditional technique with pop gloss

Robert Normand (149–150 galerie de Valois) inaugural retail space for the singular knits and graphic designs of the thirtysomething Frenchman who has worked with Lanvin, Pucci and Christophe Lemaire

Pierre Hardy (156 galerie de Valois) architect-designed space for Hardy's refined men's and women's shoes

Elsewhere

Agnès B, 2,3,6& 19 rue du Jour, 1er top-drawer brand for basics and

shop…

classics. Branches citywide and world-wide.

Antoine, 10 avenue de l'Opéra, 1er
umbrellas of quality

Charvet, 28 place Vendôme, 1er
maker of bespoke and off-the-peg
men's shirts, est. 1838

Kabuki Femme, 25 rue Etienne-Mar-cel, 1er multi-label boutique stocking
Prada, Miu Miu, Fendi bags, Miu Miu
shoes. Menswear at number 21

Maria Luisa, 7 rue Rouget de Lisle,
1er a new, pared-down flagship for
this respected boutique stocking Mc-Queen, Véronique Branquinho, Chris-topher Kane and, exclusively in Paris,
Marios Schwab and Manolo Blahnik.
Menswear round the corner at 38 rue
du Mont-Thabor

Neila, 28 rue du Mont-Thabor, 1er
fascinating vintage store with Cath-erine Deneuve-worthy stock, and JS
Bach keyboard suites on the stereo

Royal Cheese, 24 rue Tiquetonne,
2ème well-selected casualwear: Cheap
Monday, Stüssy, Edwin

Kokon To Zai, 48 rue Tiquetonne,
2ème sibling store to the original in
Soho, a similar story of look-at-me
styles and emerging designers

Repetto, 22 rue de la Paix, 2ème real
ballet pumps, as well as the madly pop-ular satin *ballerines* with outdoor soles

Rue du Mail, 5 rue du Mail, 2ème
new HQ for Martine Sitbon, mistress
of womanly glamour

Champs Elysees & Avenue Montaigne

■ Avenue des Champs Elysées, 8ème

Le66 (66) new concept boutique com-posed of transparent modules, full of
supercool books and mags, shoes and
fashion, including a section curated by
vintage store Come On Eline (16–18
rue des Taillandiers, 11ème)

Sephora (70) temple to *maquillage*.
Many branches.

Fnac (74) all the books, CDs and
DVDs you can carry, as well as audio
kit and other techy stuff. Branches all
over.

Louis Vuitton (101) sophisticated
flagship for the brand of brands, jux-taposing the fashion, jewellery and
bags with contemporary art. Also at 22
avenue Montaigne, 8ème, and 6 place
St-Germain-des-Prés, 6ème.

■ Avenue Montaigne, 8ème

Prada (10) Miuccia's essential hand-bags, shoes and prêt-à-porter clothes
collection

Joseph (14) luxury basics, black trou-sers, on-trend knitwear. Check website
for branches

Louis Vuitton (22) see Avenue des
Champs-Elysées, above

Dior (26–30) quintessentially Parisian
couture and ready-to-wear designed for
Dior by John Galliano. Dior Homme is
now helmed by Belgian Kris Van As-sche. Check website for other branches.

Celine (36) casualwear for the super-chic and the rather rich. Also at 68 rue
de Rennes, 6ème.

Chanel (42) see Rue Cambon, above.
Calvin Klein (55). All-American design-erwear.

Marni (57) feminine, sexy, wearable la-bel, especially great for dresses, sandals and chunky bangles and necklaces

Gucci (60) status-enhancing clothing and accessories from the Italians

▦ Rue du Faubourg-St-Honoré, 8ème

Lanvin (15 and 22) a temple to Alber Elbaz's intensely glamorous designs at no 22; men have their own four-storey shop over the road

La Perla (20) glamorous lingerie and swimwear. Also at 179 boulevard St-Germain, 6ème.

Hermès (24) classy – and we mean that – womenswear now overseen by the noble Jean-Paul Gaultier, as well as menswear and those wonderful leather goods. Also at 42 avenue Georges V, 8ème.

Givenchy (28) elegant womenswear with a pedigree, in a nicely art-directed new store. Also at 3 avenue Georges V, 8ème.

Roger Vivier (29) Vivier was largely credited with inventing the stiletto heel, and has shod both HM the Queen (for her coronation), and Brigitte Bardot (thigh-high boots). His name lives on, the label now looked after by Bruno Frisoni (see Rue de Grenelle, below).

Yves Saint Laurent (38) see place St-Sulpice, below

Comme des Garçons (54) a suitably high-concept boutique for the influen-tial avant-gardery of Rei Kawakubo. There's a dedicated perfume boutique at 23 place du Marché-St-Honoré.

Chloé (54–56) girlish ready-to-wear

from the classic Paris label

The Left Bank & Saint-germain-des-prés

▦ Boulevard Saint-Germain, 5eme/6ème/7ème

Diptyque (34) beautiful candles, in some 50 different scents, made with such good ingredients they perfume a room even unlit

Emporio Armani (149) affordable Armani, with a café and bookshop

La Hune (170) open late (11.45pm, Mon–Sat), this literary lair is great for vicarious intellectual experiences, aka browsing

Sonia Rykiel (175) emblematic Left Bank chic – stripy, insouciant and best accessorised with a Gauloise. Check website for other stores.

Shu Uemura (176) cult colour range, with scores of pop and neutral shades for eyes, lips and nails. The oil cleanser is a modern skincare classic.

La Perla (179) see Rue du Faubourg-St-Honoré, above

Alexandra Sojfer (218) fashionable umbrellas, parasols and canes, both antique and new

▦ Rue de Grenelle, 6ème/7ème

Yohji Yamamoto (3) the abstract silhouette of Yohji clothes is beautiful, dignified and interesting: perfect for the mature woman with deep pockets and an independent mind

Martin Margiela (13) understated yet detailed fashion for women and men

shop...

183

from the anonymous Belgian. Also at 23 & 25 bis, rue de Montpensier, 1er.

Iris (28) shoe boutique with lines from Marc Jacobs, Chloé, Viktor & Rolf and Paul Smith

Miu Miu (16) see Rue St-Honoré, above

Charles Jourdan (17) eternally foxy, elegant shoes for getting that *haute bourgeoisie* look

Carine Gilson (18) very sophisticated, hand-finished silk lingerie

Sergio Rossi (22) sexy Italian killer shoes

Bruno Frisoni (24) unconventional and innovative shoes, albeit superglam

Editions de Parfums Frédéric Malle (37) elite perfumer, whose scents are as desirable as they are modish.

Christian Louboutin (38) young pretender to the Blahnik throne, creator of red-soled seductress kit, shoemaker to the stars

---

■ Rue Bonaparte, 6ème

Assouline (35) publishers' outlet, specialising in art, photography, design and fashion volumes

Mona (17) much-loved boutique with a well-edited selection of Chloé, Alaïa, Lanvin and so on

Princesse Tam Tam (53) cute and sexy lingerie and swimwear at realistic prices

Comptoir des Cotonniers (59) demure, wearable mid-market womenswear. Also at 33 rue des Francs-Bourgeois, 4ème and citywide.

Cacharel (64) updated girlie-chic label specialising in quirky, quality pieces

Joseph (68–70) chic and classic women's wear for both daytime and evening. A fantastic range of coats.

■ Rue des Saints-Pères, 6ème/ 7ème

Paul & Joe (62) the hip end of mid-market fashion: retro-styled pieces for cool twentysomethings

Sabbia Rosa (73) irresistible satin, silk and chiffon negligées and lingerie, and those feather-trimmed mules we girls like to relax in

---

■ Boulevard Raspail, 7ème

Paul Smith (22) quirky English style exported. Also at 3 rue du Faubourg St-Honoré.

L'Artisan Parfumeur (24) heady scents (Premier Figuier is our favourite) and good-quality candles

---

Elsewhere

Georges de Providence, 3 rue de Fleurus, 6ème very cool independent shop stocking design and furniture alongside niche fashion brands such as Kitsuné and Robert Normand

Lagerfeld Gallery, 40 rue de Seine, 6ème a shop designed by Andrée Putman for the Chanel head honcho to house a selection of his own-name designs, and lots of photographs and books (he is nuts about both). See also **Kaiser Karl's 7L bookshop**, 7 rue de Lille, 7ème.

Marie-Hélene de Taillac, 8 rue de

Tournon, 6ème fabulous precious and semi-precious stones set with imaginative creativity. Big treatsville.

Vanessa Bruno, 25 rue Saint-Sulpice, 6ème fluid, flattering, feminine pieces that are cool *and* sexy. Branches in the 1st and 3rd arrondissements.

Yves Saint Laurent, 6 place Saint-Sulpice 6ème Stéphane Pilati is the custodian of the YSL legend. The boutique was refitted in bold red in 2008, the year of the designer's death. Menswear at no 12; also at at 32 and 28, rue du Faubourg-St-Honoré, 8ème.

Marais

▓ Rue des Francs Bourgeois, 4ème

Kiehl's (15) high-quality beauty products from the New York brand

Comptoir des Cotonniers (33) see Rue Bonaparte, above

Zadig & Voltaire (42) elegant basics and quirky cashmere casualwear

▓ Rue Vieille du Temple, 3ème/4eme

Nodus (22) men's shirts, from classic plain white to dandy stripes and checks

Iro (53) one of the talked-about youth brands of the moment, supplying skinny jeans, fashiony knits and leather jackets. Branch at 68 rue des St-Pères, 6ème.

Jamin Puech (68) boho bags from now-established eponymous pair

Manoush (75) boho-wear for girls who do colours, including party-destined sparkly shoes

Yukiko (97) classic vintage, offbeat originals and customised in-betweens

APC (112) hip basics. Anglo-Saxons can't believe the French have APC, when we get M&S and the Gap. Stands for Atelier de Production et Création, by the way. Also at 38 rue Madame, 6ème, and 5 rue de Marseille, 10ème. See below for the surplus store in Montmartre.

Galerie Simon (124) young global fashion talent, sourced and showcased, focusing on the ethical and the original

▓ Rue de Charlot, 3ème

Le Bouclard (15) well-heeled streetwear

Jack Henry (25) impeccably crafted, celebral womenswear, and Paris-made bags and jewellery

AB33 (30) multi-label boutique with a young mindset, stocking Vanessa Bruno and Laundry Industry

Julien, Caviste (50) small, independent wine merchant, promoting small, independent makers

Gaspard Yurkievich (43) avant-garde, detailed fashion for men and women. Also recommended for shoe fetishists.

Corinne Cobson (66) contemporary rock-chic collections

Surface to Air (68) Raf by Raf Simons, B-Store, Alice McCall… quite Lower East Side, in the Haut Marais. It's not just a concept store; it's a creative agency, too.

Les Belles Images (74) men's and women's boutique with emerging names in among the Westwood and Eley Kishimoto

■ Rue du Poitou, 3ème

Le Belle Epoque (10) vintage, with lots of daring 1970s pieces; owner Philippe knows the story behind every playsuit and pair of platforms

Shine (15) one of the newer, younger multi-brand boutiques, stocking desirables form Acne Jeans, Cheap Monday, Earl Jean, Marc by Marc Jacobs, See by Chloé and Repetto pumps

Swildens (22) easy chic pieces from a young French designer, patronised by Carla Bruni, among others

Violette & Léonie (27) new in 2009, a browsable fashion emporium with vintage and new designs, and an online shop (www.violetteetleonie.com)

Christophe Lemaire (28) new boutique devoted to own-label menswear by the Lacoste designer, designed to feel like a well-appointed apartment

Jacenko (38) good mix of casual and tailoring for men from John Smedley, Viktor & Rolf and English up-and-comer Holland Esquire

■ Rue de Saintonge, 3ème

Pretty Box (46) recent vintage

Isabel Marant (47) highly wearable womenswear, from body-con to boho, arrayed in a cabin-style shop interior

Dolls (56) hip source for labels such as Sass & Bide and By Malene Birger

April 77 (49) cult jeans label beloved of the young and skinny

Elsewhere

Antik Batik, 18 rue Turenne, 4ème kaftans and other gauzy prints

Azzedine Alaïa, 4 rue de Moussy, 4ème Paris HQ of the Tunisian legend, beloved of glamorous amazons

L'Eclaireur, 3 rue des Rosiers, 4ème amazing, ever-growing empire of boutiques, selling accessories and design, as well as as pieces by Dries Van Noten, Undercover, Sonia Rykiel and Sinha-Stanic. L'Eclaireur Homme is at 12 rue **Malher,** 4ème. Check website for other branches. The one at 10 rue Hérold, 1er, is filled with all sorts of weird and wonderful objets and artist's furniture.

Free 'P' Star, 8 rue Sainte-Croix-de-la-Bretonnerie, 4ème popular and affordable vintage clothing

I Love My Blender, 36 rue du Temple, 3ème fun, inviting bookshop that stocks English-language fiction, non-fiction and children's books, and French translations thereof

K Jacques, 16 rue Pavée, 4ème leather sandals from St Tropez

Mariage Frères, 30 and 35 rue du Bourg Tibourg, 4ème tea merchants extraordinaire. See Snack for more details.

Merci, 111 bvd Beaumarchais, 3ème former rag-trade factory, now a fashion/design store with a used-book bit and a flower stall, with all profits going to a children's charity in Madagascar. V cool.

Montmartre & Canal St-Martin

▓ Rue la Vieuville, 18ème

Spree (16) a favourite concept store, run by genial artist Bruno, who stocks Notify jeans, Isabel Marant, Hauschka skincare, own-brand ballet pumps and cult books and furrniture

Comme Des Garçons Pocket (17) fun, dinky Comme outlet

▓ Quai de Valmy, 10ème

Art Azart (10) art bookshop with a fine selection of fashion mags

Stella Cadente (93) colourful, girlie dresses, knits and accessories

Antoine et Lili (95) fluid, colourful clothing, childrenswear and home-wares, behind a series of candy-coloured canalside shopfronts

▓ Rue Beaurepaire, 10ème

American Apparel (10) cotton tees, sports basics and underwear in many colours, for boys and girls. Branches citywide.

Boutique Renhsen (22) skinny jeans for boys and girls

▓ Elsewhere

No Good Store, 52 rue de Martyrs, 9ème well-priced local boutique with vintage and new (emerging designers from France, Japan and the US) over two floors

Wochdom, 72 rue Condorcet, 9ème vintage for girls, mainly from the 1980s.

APC Surplus, 18 rue André de Sarte, 18ème smashing prices on men's and women's styles

Pinel, 5 rue de Cyrano de Bergerac, 18ème wonderful luxury luggage, trunks and leather goods

Tati, 4 boulevard de Rochechouart, 18ème pile-it-high department store for disposable style

Loulou Les Ames Arts, 104 quai de Jemmapes, 10ème HQ of a local photographer, who sells her own B&W prints, also found postcards and some nice junk.

Viveka Bergstrom, 23 rue de la Grange aux Belles, 10ème bold, idiosyncratic jewellery

Department Stores

▓ Le Bon Marché
24 rue de Sèvres, 7ème
Tel: 01 44 39 80 00
www.treeslbm.com
Open: 10am–7.30pm Mon–Wed; 10am–9pm Thur; 10am–8pm Fri; 9.30am–8pm Sat

The oldest department store in Paris and also the most fabulous. The fashion selections are amazing and cover it all from Chanel to Comptoir des Cotonniers. Top-drawer menswear, too, but the most exciting bit has to be the Grande Epicerie food hall on the ground floor. Worth booking a furnished rental for, just so you can cook.

shop…

Drugstore Publicis

133 avenue des Champs-Élysées, 8ème
Tel: 01 44 43 79 00
www.publicisdrugstore.com
Open: 8am–2am Mon–Fri; 10am–2pm Sat–Sun

A Paris institution whose 2004 reincarnation took everyone by surprise, Drugstore Publicis is half WH Smith, half concept store, a buzzy, highbrow mini-mall selling magazines, a bookshop, snazzy beauty counter, tabac,. wine shop, deli and pharmacy. There's also a brasserie and restaurant.

Galeries Lafayette

40 boulevard Haussmann, 9ème
Tel: 01 42 82 34 56
www.galerieslafayette.com
Open: 9.30am–8pm (9.30pm Thurs).
Closed Sundays.

Mid-revamp, the Galeries Lafayette is already coming on strong as a luxury retail event. The four stores – Lafayette Homme (menswear), Lafayette Gourmet (food), Lafayette Maison (homeware) and Lafayette Mode (fashion) – come with little extras, such as personal shopping and free fashion shows (check website for details), a sushi bar, café and champagne bar.

Printemps

64 boulevard Haussmann, 9ème
Tel: 01 42 82 50 00
www.printemps.com
Open: 9.35am–8pm (10pm Thurs).
Closed Sundays.

Competing furiously with its neighbour

Galeries Lafayette, Printemps majors in fashion, and gets particular kudos for its up-to-date jeans brands, international designers and an entire floor dedicated to the shoe. You'll also find 200 beauty brands, a tearoom, sushi bar and an Alain Ducasse café.

Markets

Marché Bastille

11ème
Open: 7am–2.30pm Thur;
7am–3pm Sun

Good, big, bustling farmers' market between rue Amelot and rue St-Sabin, with more than 100 stalls selling organic meat and veg, wet fish, great bread and regional cheeses.

Marché des Enfants Rouges

3ème
Open: 8.30am–1pm, 4–7.30pm (8pm Fri/Sat) Tues–Sat; 8.30am–2pm Sun

An organic-leaning food market on the Rue de Bretagne, a covered market since the 1770s, and back on track after petering out in the 1990s. Best on Saturday and Sundays, it's open Tuesday to Friday as well, with lots of *traiteurs* selling prepared food, and a wine bar serving oysters at weekends.

Marché aux Puces Clignancourt

north of Paris
Open: 7am–7.30pm Sat–Mon

The dealers have done all the hard

work here, and prices are high, but it's worth coming to explore the labyrinth (it's actually about ten markets in one) and toy with the idea of buying something big and impractical to drag home. You will find genuine gems (many antique shops sell beautifully restored pieces), along with the usual bric-à-brac.

Marché aux Puces de Montreuil
east of Paris
Open: 7am–7pm Sat–Mon

Stacks of second-hand tat, with some retro stalls, but the real satisfaction comes from digging out a treasure of your own. Lots of old clothes, household bits and pieces, hardware and assorted unidentifiable whatnots and thingamys.

Marché aux Puces de Vanves
14ème
Open: 7am–1pm Sat–Sun

A bit gentler than Clignancourt, ie: you are likely to actually pick up a bargain here. It's also smaller and less confusing. On a sunny day, wandering down the tree-lined street, stopping off to listen to some vintage vinyl or to try on a 1920s hats, is a real joy.

Marché aux Puces Saint-Ouen
north of Paris
Open: 9.30am–6pm Sat–Mon

An old-school market, made up of half a dozen or so divisions, from the junk stalls of Jules-Vallès, to Dauphine, where the 18th-century specialists gather, and Serpette, where dealers come to find in-demand 1950s and 1960s merchandise.

Marché Raspail
6ème
Open: 8.30am–2pm Sun

Bobo-friendly organic food market, set put between Rue du Cherche-Midi and Rue de Rennes. It's a lovely Sunday ritual to come for a stroll (and some bustling and queuing) and sample the wares. You'll want to take it all home: lavender-scented soap, honey, *saucisson*… It's also great for a wholesome brunch or lunch on the hoof.

shop…

play...

Wholesome pursuits? Paris? But of course: man cannot live by wine and fine art alone. The city is awash with sporty, healthy pleasures, from its seven racetracks to its dozens of spas and beauty salons. Simply walking around the arrondissements is perhaps the number-one way to experience the city, but you can also rollerblade en masse in the moonlight, sunbathe on the city-centre beach in midsummer, or pay just two or three euros to swim in an Art Deco pool.

As sport fans will know, Paris hosts some major events and tournaments. In early spring, the national rugby union team play their home games in the Six Nations Championship at the Stade de France in Saint Denis (built for the 1998 football World Cup Final). In May, the Stade Roland Garros hosts the French Open tennis tournament. And every July, roaring crowds, President and all, line the Champs-Elysées to see the finish of the biggest race in cycling, the Tour de France. Details of all these and more appear in France's bestselling national sports paper, L'Equipe.

Away from the big time, Paris is wonderful for the kind of spectator sports you don't have to queue for, such as watching skateboarders at the Bastille, or picking up tips from old-timers playing pétanque in the park. There's much else to learn: you'll be fed with all sorts of historical bits and pieces on a guided walk; and keen cooks – amateur or professional – can take classes in everything from market shopping to *millefeuille* engineering. Even going for a run here can double up as psychogeographical exploration, especially if you opt for a few laps around the Champs de Mars or the Jardin de Tuileries. Indoors, how about a couple of hands of poker in a wood-panelled casino? Or a sweaty bikram-yoga session (English spoken)?

Finally, in terms of spas and salons, we'll happily defer to the Parisians; they're convincingly serious about their health and beauty regimes, and the sheer number of grand hotels, prestigious brands and expert individuals competing for your euros means standards are high and the choice of styles compendious. We've listed just a handful in this section; many of our favoured hotels have excellent spas, too, from the new Carita den at Pavillon de la Reine to the world-class facilities at Park Hyatt Vendôme.

Casinos

Though it is possible in Paris simply to turn up at a casino and play, you need to carry your passport with you in order to do so. It's also advisable to don something elegant, since smarter casinos do not allow jeans or trainers. There will also sometimes be an entry charge to the games room.

Aviation Club de France
104 avenue des Champs-Elysées, 8ème
Tel: 01 45 63 32 91
www.aviationclubdefrance.com

Open 24 hours a day, seven days a week, this super-central, upscale wood-panelled club offers blackjack, baccarat, backgammon and poker and backgammon. It hosts weekly poker tournaments, and several annual tournaments, including the poker Grand Prix de Paris, which concludes with a four-day, no-limit Texas Holdem championship.

Cercle Clichy Montmartre
84, rue de Clichy, 9ème
Tel: 01 48 78 32 85
www.academie-billard.com
Open: daily, 4pm–6am

An historic, fine-looking pool hall with decorative frescos and a friendly atmosphere, which has begun to run poker tournaments over the past few years.

Cookery Courses

L'Atelier des Chefs
10 rue de Penthièvre, 8ème
Tel: 01 53 30 05 82
www.atelierdeschefs.com

Hands-on classes led by restaurant chefs, including lunchtime courses that are mobbed by working Parisians. Expect a state-of-the-art kitchen and seasonal, sophisticated menus.

Ecole du Cordon Bleu
8 rue Léon Delhomme, 15ème
Tel: 01 53 68 22 50
www.lcbparis.com

One of the three serious culinary schools in Paris, where aspiring professionals can study for a diploma in haute cuisine or pâtisserie. Amateurs can join in, too, on workshops and market tours.

Patricia Wells
rue Jacob, 6ème
www.patriciawells.com

The Paris premises of the highly respected cookery writer, who also teaches in Provence. Select, expensive and aimed at home cooks, the courses are in English, and offer terrific insights into foodie Paris.

Cycling

The Vélib' (see below) has turned the city onto two-wheels-good in a big way. Whether you're on a Vélib' or something a bit sportier, cycling can be a fun way to see the city, especially if you get out of the car-choked centre and head for the Canal St Martin or, especially at weekends, the Bois de Vincennes or Bois de Boulogne, both of which have many miles of cycle lanes. (Taking your bike on the métro is a squeeze, so be prepared to pedal to get there.) Cycling in the centre of town also becomes nicer on Sundays and public holidays, when Mayor Delanoë's de-congestion measures mean that many roads are closed to motorised traffic.

Gepetto et Vélos
59 rue du Cardinal Lemoine, 5ème
Tel: 01 43 54 19 95
www.gepetto-et-velos.com
Open: 9am–1pm, 2–7.30pm.
Closed Mondays.

This shop rents out bicycles, as well as selling BMX and Chopper-type cycles.

Paris à Vélo C'est Sympa
22 rue Alphonse Baudin, 11ème
Tel: 01 48 87 60 01
www.parisvelosympa.com

Tours by day and night, also bicycle and tandem hire. Closed Tuesdays. See also Tours.

Festivals

Bastille Day
The city is transformed into something of a street party on Le Quatorze Juillet, when the French celebrate the 1789 revolution and the birth of the republic. Military parades and crowds give way to partying and fireworks after dark.

Fashion Week
The twice-yearly shows aren't something we'd coinciding with unless you've got to be, but it's as well to know that March and October can be tricky for booking hotels and restaurants.

Fête du Travail
On May Day, everyone downs tools and spends time with family and friends. Shops and many museums and restaurants close for the day, and lily-of-the-valley (*muguet*) is sold on every corner. 2010 and 2011 are a bit of a swizz, with May Day falling on a Saturday and Sunday, respectively.

Gyms & Sports Clubs

Club Quartier Latin
19 rue de Pontoise, 5ème
Tel: 01 55 42 77 88
www.clubquartierlatin.com
Open: daily, 9am–midnight (7pm Sat/Sun)

Close to the university, with a great swimming pool (see below), four squash courts, gym facilities and classes (yoga, body sculpt, 'abdos fessiers', etc). From about €20.

play…

Espace Vit'Halles

48 rue Rambuteau, 3ème
Tel: 01 42 77 21 71 www.vithalles.com
Open: 8am–10.30pm Mon–Fri; 9am–
10pm Sat; 10am–7pm Sun

Excellent gym next to the Pompidou
Centre, with Technogym equipment,
sauna and terrific classes. From about
€25.

Horse-racing

The key date in the flat-racing calen-
dar is the prestigious Prix de l'Arc de
Triomphe Lucien Barrière, aka l'Arc,
which takes place at the Longchamp
racetrack, every October. Women in
head-turning hats get in for nothing.
The Hippodrome d'Auteuil plays host
to the Grand Steeple-chase de Paris every May. Trotting races take place in the
evenings at the Hippodrome de Paris-
Vincennes, where the Prix Amérique
has taken place every January since
1920. There are four other racetracks
around the city – but no bookies! It was
decreed in 1891 that the industry be
run under a state-associated monopoly,
to preempt corruption, so all books in
France are run by Pari-Mutuel Urbain.
So, if you fancy a flutter you simply
have to head for one of the many bars
or cafés that display the green PMU
sign outside.

Hippodrome d'Auteuil

route des Lacs, Bois de Boulogne, 16th
Tel: 01 40 71 47 47

Hippodrome de Longchamp

route des Tribunes, Bois de Boulogne,
16th
Tel: 01 44 30 75 00

Hippodrome de Paris-Vincennes

2 route de la Ferme, 12th.
Tel: 01 49 77 17 17

Ice-skating

Between December and March, the
town hall pays for several spectacular
ice rinks to be set up around the city,
including a big and ritzy one at the
l'Hôtel de Ville, and another by the
Tour Montparnasse. If you feel like
it for some reason, you can ice-skate
almost all year round (except July and
August) at the Patinoire Sonja Henie in
the Palais Omni-Sports de Paris-Bercy.

Paris-plage

The mayoral Paris-Plage wheeze sees
several stretches of the Seine sandified
for the people during July and August.
Anyone can go along to grab a sun-
lounger or hammock or take a dip in
the 28-metre pool. Open daily 8am–
midnight. See www.paris.fr for details.

Parks

You can't have everything, and what
Paris hasn't got are many central green
spaces. On the edge of the city, the
Bois de Boulogne (to the west) and
Bois de Vincennes (to the east) are
three and four times bigger than Hyde

Park respectively. The Jardin des Tuileries is an elegant promenade with bronzes, ponds and a summer funfair, between the Louvre and Place de la Concorde. Historically the king's medicine cupboard, the Jardin des Plantes in the 5th arrondissement, has winter gardens, alpine gardens and rose gardens, as well as tropical greenhouses. The biggest park within the city limits, the Jardin de Luxembourg is a 60-acre playground for *le tout Paris*, and particularly frolicsome for families. Sitting on the the the grass is forbidden (and they're watching you!), but there are plenty of cast-iron benches among the formal terraces, parterres and English gardens. Another favourite fresh-air spot is the Parc des Buttes Chaumont in the 19th, wild and steep, with intriguing paths, waterfalls and fine views.

Rollerblading

The tremendous Friday night street skate organised by Pari-Roller (www.pari-roller.com) regularly sees 15,000 rollerbladers gliding communally round the city for three hours, setting off from place Raoul Dautry, near the Tour Montparnasse, at 10pm. The skill and speed of those taking part are impressive so, honestly, don't bother unless you've got the moves. There are marshals and a police escort but it's free to take part unless you want to pay a subscription that includes insurance. During the day on Sundays, there's a more relaxed skate run by Rollers et Coquillages (www.rollers-coquillages. org). Alternatively, the stretch of the Left Bank from the Musée d'Orsay to the Eiffel Tower is blader central on Sundays between 9am and 5pm, when it's closed to traffic. See below for suggested skate-hire shop.

Roller Location Nomade
37 boulevard Bourdon, 4ème
Tel: 01 44 54 07 44
www.nomadeshop.com

Running

The embankments of the Seine and the perimeters of the Champ-de-Mars are popular jogging spots, as are the Jardin du Luxembourg, the Jardin des Plantes and the Tuileries. Running up the Canal St Martin to the Parc de la Villette is great if you're based around there. A little further afield, the Bois de Boulogne and the Bois de Vincennes are excellent for longer, scenic runs. The Hash House Harriers, a group who describe themselves as a drinking club with a running problem, organise weekly runs (www.parishhh.free.fr). The Paris Marathon takes place every April (www.parismarathon.com), and the half-marathon in March.

Spas & Beauty Salons

Anne Semonin
Hôtel Le Bristol,
112 rue du Faubourg-St-Honoré, 8ème
Tel: 01 53 43 43 00
www.annesemonin.com
Open: 10am–7pm. Closed Sundays.

Highly effective, traditional treatments in a sleek setting (quite a contrast to Le Bristol's chintzy public spaces),

play…

including lymphatic drainage and Bastien pedicures, from experienced staff. Anne Semonin products use essential oils wisely to benefit sensitive skin.

L'Appartement 217
217 rue Saint-Honoré, 1er
Tel: 01 42 96 00 96
www.lappartement217.com
Open: 10am–7pm. Closed Mondays and Tuesdays.

Stéphane Jaulin, formerly in charge of the beauty corner at Colette (see Shop), had this Haussmannian apartment well and truly feng shui'd (nice colours!) before setting up his organic spa. His cutting-edge therapies range from Skin Oxygen Therapy to the Physio-Harmonising Massage, and weight loss via the mysterious Iyashi Dôme.

Les Bains du Marais
31 rue des Blancs Manteaux, 4ème
Tel: 01 44 61 02 02
www.lesbainsdumarais.com

A *hammam* and spa in the Marais, serving mint tea and offering the traditional *gommage* cleansing massage, as well as various other beauty treatments. Ring to check opening times.

Boutique Clarins
10 rue de Babylone, 8ème
Tel: 01 45 44 06 19 www.clarins.com
Open: 9.15am–7.15pm. Closed Sundays.

Men and women's treatments, including special packages for expectant and new mothers, are on offer in this small but excellent spa, done out in Clarins' signature red and white.

Guerlain
68 avenue des Champs-Elysées, 8ème
Tel: 01 45 62 52 57
www.guerlain.com
Open: daily, 10.30am–8pm Mon–Sat; 3–7pm Sun

The HQ of this historic perfumers is truly dazzling, following a gilded revamp in 2005. It's high on the sightseeing list, and an irresistible showcase for Guerlain's wonderful scents; the beauty centre is good for facials and for learning cunning skincare techniques.

Institut Dior
Plaza Athenée,
25 avenue Montaigne, 8ème
Tel: 01 53 67 66 65 www.dior.com
Open: 8am–10pm. Closed Sundays.

The pale Dior palette of the luxy spa in the basement of the Plaza Athénée has a lovely soothing effect, especially for guests of the hotel, who can melt directly into their rooms following a massage or facial. If you're not staying, plan to pause a while after your treatment, to make the most of the dove-grey relaxation space.

Nickel
48 rue des Francs Bourgeois, 3ème
Tel: 01 42 77 41 10
www.nickel.fr
Open: 11am–7.30pm (9pm Weds/ Thurs). Closed Sundays.

A pioneering men-only spa, and not entirely angled towards a gay clientele, in spite of its Marais location, Nickel has grown into a global skincare brand. The spa offers face and body treatments, waxing, and packages that combine them all.

Nuxe Spa

32 rue Montorgueil, 1er
Tel: 01 55 80 71 40 www.nuxe.com
Open: 9am–9pm (7.30pm Sat). Closed Sundays.

A welcoming, discreet, super-central space, with wenge wood and polished concrete lending an air of contemporary luxury. Natural ingredients are key to Nuxe products and treatments, with honey, plant extracts and essential oils on the menu.

Swimming

All pools require you to wear a swimming cap, and men must wear snug, Speedo-type swimming trunks – none of your forgiving Vilebrequins. Entrance to public pools is set at €2.60, or you can get a 10-visit pass for €21.50. Ring to check times.

Aquaboulevard

4 rue Louis Armand, 15th
Tel: 01 40 60 10 00

This enormous privately run complaex is perfect for children, thanks to year-round heating, wave machines and waterslides. It also has three saunas and a steam bath.

Piscine Butte-aux-Cailles

5 place Paul Verlaine, 13ème
Tel: 01 45 89 60 05

A wonderful red-brick Art Deco building dating from 1924, its highlight the 25-metre outdoor pool filled with naturally warm water from an artesian well at the site. There are two outdoor pools, too, open in summer

Piscine Georges Vallerey

148 avenue Gambetta, 20ème
Tel: 01 40 31 15 20

A big pool with a retractable roof, sun-beds, a bar area and a children's pool. It was built for the 1924 Olympics and Tarzan actor Johnny Weissmuller used to come and train here.

Piscine Josephine Baker

quai François-Mauriac, 13th
Tel: 01 44 68 12 12

Just near the National Library, this pool is suspended in the water of the Seine; it has two big sundecks, one of them on the roof of the pool itself, as well as a sauna, gym and café.

Piscine Pontoise Quartier Latin

19 rue de Pontoise, 5ème
Tel: 01 55 42 77 88
www.clubquartierlatin.com

A gem of Art Deco design near the Sorbonne, with mosaics, columns and original brass fittings. A glass roof lets in natural light. On week nights the pool is open till 11.45pm for evening sessions. The gym is excellent, too (see above).

Piscine Suzanne Berlioux
10 place de la Rotonde,
Forum des Halles, 1er
Tel: 01 42 36 98 44

This underground swimming complex is one of Paris' most central, and contains a 50-metre pool that's great for lap swimming. The windows on one side give onto a tropical greenhouse.

Tours

Canauxrama
13 quai de la Loire, 19ème
Tel: 01 42 39 15 00
www.canauxrama.fr

The Bateaux-Mouches are the classic way to experience Paris afloat; for a change, you could spend two and a half hours scooting gently up the Canal St-Martin, €14.

City-bird
Tel: 08 26 10 01 00
www.city-bird.com

It sounds adrenalin-charged but, really, the point of this guided tour by motorbike isn't speed – it's ease of passage. Still great fun, though,from €70.

Fat Tire Bike Tours
Tel: 01 56 58 10 54
www.fattirebiketoursparis.com

Bike hire, and tours of Paris, Giverny and Versailles, as well as night tours, leaving from the base of the Eiffel Tower. They also offer Segway tours – but really! See also Cycling.

Paris Walking Tours
Tel: 01 48 09 21 40
www.paris-walks.com

Wised-up expats lead groups entertainingly around the Marais and Latin Quarter, leaving at 10.30am and 2.30pm daily. From €10.

Velib'

Naysayers have been silenced by the success of the city's Vélib' scheme, which was launched in 2007. Basically, 20,000 commuter bikes are stationed around the city, each locked to its stand until someone comes along to release it with a credit card. They're only meant for short journeys; once you've got from A to B (€1 for half an hour), you replace it on another stand elsewhere. It's a joy to watch clubbers wobbling home on the sturdy grey bikes at 4am, and commuters trundling along in the mornings, all part of a happy, environmentally sensible social experiment. Tourists can use them, too – you just need a chip-and-pin credit/debit card to release one from its stand or *borne*. The only bind is turning up somewhere where all the stands are occupied, and having to pay an overtime penalty. Codes and etiquettes have sprung up (if the saddle's the wrong way round, the bike needs repairing), and the scheme is widely considered a Good Thing.

Yoga

Bikram Yoga Paris
13 rue Simon Le Franc, 4ème
Tel: 01 42 47 18 52
www.bikramyogaparis.com

There's a daily class in English at this 'hot yoga' studio, which has a second location in the 9th arrondissement. From €25.

Rasa Yoga
21 rue Saint Jacques, 5ème
Tel: 01 43 54 14 52
www.rasa-yogarivegauche.com

Iyengar, Ashtanga, Mysore-style Ashtanga, Kundalini and prenatal classes, also a wonderful range of massage techniques. From €20.

notes...

info…

Arrondissements

The 20 postal-code districts of Paris spiral out snailwise from the 1st/1er/*premier arrondissement* on the Right Bank. The last two digits of a postal code indicate the arrondissement, for example: an address with the postal code of 75003 is in the 3ème. Note that the arrondissements (it means, literally, 'rounding') don't correspond with areas' names precisely.

August, etc

Everyone takes a two-week holiday in August, and many, but not all restaurants, bars, clubs and shops will shut for the whole of the month, so the city is almost sleepy, which can be quite nice. There are many bank holidays around Easter and in May; and Sunday is a day of rest, when shops and many cafés and restaurants close, though the Marais tends to stay open for shopping.

Emergency numbers:

Ambulance (SAMU): 15
Police :17
Fire (sapeurs-pompiers): 18
Emergency (from a mobile): 112
24-hour pharmacy: Derhy, 84 avenue des Champs-Elysées.
American Hospital in Paris (private): 01 46 41 25 25

Métro

Cheap and easy, the underground system has numbered lines, with each direction named after the last stop. Trains run from 5.30am to 12.40 in the week, and till 1.30am Friday–Sunday. The five RER lines run through Paris and out into the suburbs and can be useful for speeding across town. You're best off buying a carnet of 10 tickets for €11.40; you can get these at *métro* stations and *tabacs*. Hold onto your ticket till you're out of the station, in case of spot checks.

Money

The currency is the euro (€).

Smoking

Paris is a city of smokers, as you will observe, but smoking is now banned in all public places in France, though smoking rooms are allowed in clubs and bars, subject to strict rules. Cigarettes are sold in *tabacs*.

Taxis

It isn't easy to hail a cab on the streets; instead, make your way to a taxi rank, marked with a blue sign. Ideally, keep a map on you, as cab-drivers here aren't as expert at finding addresses as you'd hope. There is a minimum charge of €5.60, and most trips in central Paris should cost somewhere between €8 and €15. From Orly Airport, it's about €50; from Charles de Gaulle, €50–€70. Don't be surprised by the luggage surcharge, €1 a piece. If you want a receipt, ask for *la note*. N.B.: a white light on the roof means the car is free; the similar-to-the-novice orange light means it is taken.

Taxis Bleus

Tel: 01 49 36 10 10 www.taxis-bleus.com

Taxis G7

Tel: 01 47 39 47 39 www.taxis-g7.fr

Telephone

The international dialling code for France is +33. The local code for Paris is 01, and the 01 is part of the number when you're calling a local number within Paris. Make sure you drop the '0' when dialling France from abroad, ie: +33 1…

Tickets

FNAC (see Shop) is the best place to buy tickets for gigs, etc. *Pariscope*, published weekly on a Wednesday, carries listings of what's on. For an English-language listing, see www.parisinfo.com, which also gives box-office telephone numbers and online booking links. The main tourist office is at 99 rue de Rivoli, 1er. To avoid horrid queuing, you can get a Paris Museum Pass (www.parismuseumpass.com), also available at participating museums or the tourist office, from €30 for two days of unlimited access, no waiting, to more than 60 cultural sites in and around Paris.

Tipping

In France, a service charge of 10–15 per cent is included in your bill by law at restaurants, cafés and bars, but do as the Parisians do, and round up the bill to the nearest euro, adding a couple more for luck after a good meal.

index...

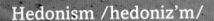

Hedonism /hedoniz'm/

*"The philosophy that pleasure is the highest
good and proper aim of human life."*
– Oxford English Dictionary

Hg2 Corporate

Branded Gifts....

Looking for a corporate gift with real value? Want to reinforce your company's presence at a conference or event? We can provide you with branded guides so recipients will explore their chosen city with your company's logo right under their nose.

Branding can go from a small logo discreetly embossed on to our standard cover, to a fully custom jacket in your company's colours and in a material of your choice. We can also include a letter from your CEO/Chairman/President and add or remove as much or as little other content as you require. We can create a smaller, 'best of' guide, branded with your company's livery in a format of your choice. Custom guides can also be researched and created from scratch to any destination not yet on our list.

For more information, please contact Ben at ben@hg2.com

Content licensing....

We can also populate your own website or other materials with our in-depth content, superb imagery and insider knowledge.

For more information, please contact Tremayne at tremayne@hg2.com

Hg2|New York Hg2|Milan Hg2|Dubai Hg2|Paris

Hg-Who?

Welcome to the world of Hg2 – the UK's leading luxury city guide series. Launched in 2004 as the *A Hedonist's guide to…* series, we are pleased to announce a new look to our guides, now called simply Hg2. In response to customer feedback, the new Hg2 is 25% lighter, even more luxurious to look at or touch, and flexible, for greater portability. However, fear not, our content is still as meticulously researched and well-illustrated as ever and the spirit of hedonism still infuses our work. Our brand of hedonism taps into the spirit of 'Whatever Works for You' – from chic boutique hotels to well-kept-secret restaurants, to the very best cup of coffee in town. We do not mindlessly seek out the most expensive; instead, we search high and low for the very best each city has to offer.

So take Hg2 as your companion to a city. Written by well-regarded journalists and constantly updated online at www.Hg2.com (register this guide to get one year of free access), it will help you Sleep, Eat, Drink, Shop, Party and Play like a sophisticated local.

"Hg2 is about foreign life as art" **Vanity Fair**
"The new travel must-haves" **Daily Telegraph**
"Insight into what's really going on" **Tatler**
"A minor bible" **New York Times**
"Excellent guides for stylish travellers" **Harper's Bazaar**
"Discerning travellers, rejoice!" **Condé Nast Traveller**